FARMDALE BOYS

I0149900

ANTHONY BROWN

Friendship Publishing

Four Friends That Turned Into Brothers

Growing up in Seattle, I had a dream of becoming a boxer, so I decided to sign up at a local gym called Raineer Gym. Right away I realized that I had extremely fast hands and devastating power. I beat everyone at my age in the gym and won my first few fights. The local papers and neighborhood started to talk about me, months later, I was scheduled to fight in a big tournament where Olympic coaches and local televisions were to be in attendance. Boy I was so excited I can remember running home to tell my mom the great news! My mothers response was " That's great son, but we're moving to California so you won't be able to attend". I was beyond hurt! I pleaded with my mom, only to be told no, In the car, on the way to California, that ride seemed like three years, I just hated every minute of it! Finally, I asked my mother what part of CA are we going to anyway!? , she replied, "COMPTON!". I said , "what kind of place is that!?". I've never heard of a place called Compton, boy was I sure to find out. the first day we arrived and after parking at the house where we were going to live I remember my mom telling me to go to the store and buy her some Cigarettes, I ask her where's the store Mom, I don't know anything about this area, she point down the street and tells me walk four block and turn right and you'll see the store in front of you, So off I went. On my way , I run into two guys on a bike. Me being from Seattle a place that's kind and friendly, I greeted the two guys, only to be greeted with a "Who you talking to Poot-but!". Not knowing what a Poot-butt meant, I kinda knew that it couldn't have been anything good, so I replied with " hey , I was only trying to be nice". Then one of the guys said "Well you talking all that shit! You boxing!? You want to thump?"

Being the square I was , I respond " Yea! I boxed", and before I knew it, the one guy hit me square in the jaw! Pow! For a second, I had no idea where I was, once I recovered, I quickly started to apply my boxing techniques , and turned the fight in my favor. I quickly learned that this was not Seattle, and the guy who was in front of me, was much tougher than anyone I fought in Seattle, roughly 10 minutes into it, I earned respect of both guys, as the fight came to an end they walked away saying , "okay nigga, you can thump!". I had forgot all about going to the store and went back home. I mean, it was my first day in Compton! Incredible! Once I arrived back home I told my Mom what had happened she replies where's the stuff I ask you to get? Never ask was I ok, just where's my stuff, that was my Mom! So the next day its time to enroll in school

 I was scheduled to enroll at elementary school called (Lincoln). The world is so different in Compton compared to Seattle. At home, the makeup of nationalities were predominantly : whites, Asians, & Samoans. In Compton, its dominated by Blacks. So this world is completely different. So my first day everything seems to be going well, pretty girls, teachers are cool, so far, no problems. My little brother and I are walking through the cafeteria, the grades are divided , first grade in this section, sixth grade in that section. So far so good. I'm seating down eating my lunch but forgot to get my drink, so I go back to the counter to retrieve my juice. On my way there, this boy in my

ANTHONY BROWN

classroom says "yea, if he keeps walking by me in class I'ma beat his ass!". Everyone at the table quickly looked and me and started saying "Oooo!". Meaning they wanted to see a Fight (instigating) and to Encourage the Kid (Name Terry)!So i turned my attention back to terry to see if he was talking to me, he Says yea Punk I'm talking to You! by this time I've already had Enough of these Wanting be tough guys from Compton!! so as he gets up from his Seat and decides to push me m thinking in my mind damn I've been here three days and I'm already involved in two fights, well i quickly made easy work of terry! A Right Cross, left over hand ! Fights Over!- Poor Terry never Had a Chance!

At the time I didn't Know Terry was considered one of the best fighters in the school so by beating him gained instant respect from the other students! It wasn't something that I wanted to do i just wanted to just blend in and be left alone but during that time in Compton where I lived it was about earning respect by your ability to go toe to toe, As we move on to Jr High school which was six months later (Roosevelt Jr High) which is five blocks down the street- Prior to graduation from Lincoln i met this kid who eventually became my best friend, (Very important later in the story)! We would hang out together and after school would walk to this local hamburger spot name Alex burgers were both of our Moms worked after graduation from Elementary school we lost contact,

Events seemed to happen often and spontaneously in Compton the summer prior to Jr. High School. My mom decided to go out on the town with her guy friend , so she asked a neighbor in the apartment building if my brother and I could stay the night and keep an eye on us. The neighbor agreed. Before I go further, it's important that I describe this neighbor, it was a 25 year old woman that every man in the neighborhood wanted. Her name was Elanor, 5'7, 38D Chest, 24 inch waist, and her Ass(Butt) should've been illegal. See they didn't have any spandex tights to hide your flaws back then, it was either you had it or you didn't, and believe me she had it all! Okay, back to the story, so my brother and I march over to Elanor's apartment, everything is going well, we're watching TV, eating taco's, it's all great. The next morning, which was about 7am, my brother and I had woke up and started to watch television Elanor walks in the living room and asks us if we want breakfast, we both said sure!

She goes back to the room and says that she'll meet us both in the kitchen. We said cool, after about 30min had gone by and we noticed she hadn't arrived, but we were patient no problem we just felt she was on the phone or something like that. Suddenly, she comes back in the kitchen with just a towel covering her chest, but because her chest was so large, it didn't cover her bottom, we looked and all we could see was this extremely hairy pussy. So as she approaches the table, my brother and I turned completely –our faces almost turned white! Man!! Look!", as I said to Alvin (brother), he says " Ooh Tony man that's her pussy showing!". Before I could respond, Elanor sticks her tongue in my ear and snatched me from the kitchen table and took me in the living room. She throws me on the couch, took off her towel , got on top of me, and grabbed my Johnson ! By this time, I'm beyond scared to death, you would think a boy would love to be in this position, normally I probably would have been if she was my age but this grown mature women with all this developed bodied I was shocked at myself for being so scared. I remember telling my brother Alvin "Man, help me!". Only to look over and watch him bent over in laughter! Because his complexion was so light he turned Red as hell and looking like Rudolph the rain deer ! Well as the moment went on, I just let the process take its course until it was finally over, needless to say, I was a completely different boy after the experience; I walked around dazed for weeks at a time at what happened. Alvin kept asking me! soo how was it ? Alvin kept saying! Tony man you was looking Kind of scared man! i just responded man! just change the subject! Yo Ass didn't try to help me so just forget it- Everything to Alvin was always funny so he just laughed!

ANTHONY BROWN

See, things like this happen to little boys all the time from Older women molesting them, most boys just don't say anything they just role with it and keep it to themselves, you begin to see it more and more these days with Teachers (Females) are having sex with Jr. High students (Who are Male) all the time now. Maybe Elanor was on drugs (red devil pill), for her to be that pretty and that well built to molest a 12 year old boy ; still baffles me to this day – the "Emergence of drugs in the Neighborhood."

Every 1st and 15th, My Mom would receive food stamps from the county as well a stipend. Those twice a month checks would not only uplift the house hold, but would bring joy and laughter through every household in the apartment Complex. Boyfriends and fathers who were normally no where to be found would always show up on the 1st and 15th to partake in the festivities associated with county checks, free loaders, drug dealers, etc. So This one guy in particular, would always try and befriend my Mom when she got her checks , I guess it was because my mom was high yellow, at that time in society, high yellow women were in high demand! I took notice of him, mainly for his cock-eye slender shady demeanor. I just had a bad feeling about him the moment I laid eyes on him. As time went on, my mom seemed to accept this guy who's name was Dexter'. I can remember him telling her, you need to try this with your drink! (Colt 45 Beer) It will only intensify your high! Turned out it was the pills (Red Devils). So she decided to try the combination! Bad Idea! Between drinking and the drugs, i began to see a change in the way my mom started to behave, it began to get the best of my mom. Several days coming home from school, my brother and I would find my mom passed out on the floor from the consumption of Alcohol and Red Devils were just not a good combination and like clockwork this Cock-eyed slithering Snake Dexter would pop up on the 1st and the 15th to make his transactions. Pills for food stamps, or cash! So This one particular day, Dexter decided to brings his brother Ronald with him for the pickup. Ronald was very tall and muscular in build, and always wore an Indian Style Vest with huge arms showing, So this one day, Dexter and Ronald come by the apartment complex, going from one apartment to another , until finally stopping at ours. Dexter tells Ronald, "Hey man, I have to make a run, hang out here until I come back". Ronald says "fine" man just hurry back. All I remember is Ronald and my mom started drinking and dropping pills before we knew it Ronald had passed out on the living room floor. So we think, no big deal, he'll get up in a few minutes, 30 minutes go by no problem we just kept going about our business, then an hour goes by then two hours, still Ronald did not get up. Suddenly we notice a pack of Red Devils and Rainbow pills in his pockets one of the neighbors who had came by our apartment said Girl this nigga may have overdosed! Panic Starts to set in because we now realize that's actually what had happed Ronald had overdosed! See when a person overdosed the philosophy was to give them milk and this would dilute the drugs and thus restore the person, so we tried several times to insert milk into Ronald's mouth ! all he would do was just throw it back up! Another neighbor had just so happen to drop by and seen us in this panic state! He took one look at Ronald and told my Mom if you don't call the Paramedics now! this Niggas Going to Die on your Floor! so my Mom did just That- When the Paramedics arrived they immediately went to work on Ronald giving him CPR!

Seconds later his Brother Dexter arrived back to my Moms only to see his brother lying on the floor fighting for his Life! Dexter Looked at my Mom and Said BITCH! if my Brother Dies I'm Killing You and Everybody in Here

"You and your whole family better hope that he lives", I've never seen my mom look so scared. She's this 5'0 , 135,lbs woman being faced with this horror of having this guy die in her apartment with his cock-eye brother standing there watching. By this time, the entire apartment building is outside watching to see what was going to happen,

ANTHONY BROWN

suddenly, by God's grace, Ronald started responding by coughing – the paramedics rush him to the hospital and he survived! By this time, I'd had enough of this Compton shit! The place was nothing like my home town of Seattle. Two days after this situation with Ronald, I went to my mom and went all in. I never cussed at my mom but I made my point loud and clear. I told her I'm through with Compton! "I'm going to live with my father!". I asked her why would she want to stay in this stupid ass place. So I go on and on about all the bad shit that happened since we arrived in this God forsaken place. Suddenly, I hear my friend calling me to come out and play football! Come on Tony Man! We want you on our team!". This went on for 5-10 minutes. When I finally said "okay, I'm coming out, I'll be there", My mom says " son sit down, I have to tell you something very important", I'm like "Mom, I love you but I can't live here with you, I hate this place, just call my father!", that's when the bombshell hit , "Son, you don't have a father, your real father died when I was pregnant with you!". She goes on to say a sailor killed him while they were fighting, by this time it felt like my heart had stopped. I then asked her "who is this nigga that comes around saying he's my father !?", she goes on to say, "that's your father's brother, he said he would pretend to be your dad until you were old enough to understand". If you ever want to take the air out of a little kid (girl or boy), tell them something like this! See, next to God, is your father; we look at him for everything! It was a very low point for me, but I managed to get up and went out to play ball with my friends that day.

If things couldn't go from bad to worse! So we go across the street to the front of Compton High School. They had two big grass fields that sat right in front of the school. No one had a football so we played with a milk carton. The object of the game was to tackle whoever had the milk carton. There were roughly 20 players who participated. Please let me say it's a rough game , because unless you have high level skills, it can get ugly! So the game starts, a player picks up the cart with the 19 guys pursuing, if you get hit you can throw the cart in the air , which frees you from getting hit and allows the other player to catch it and try his luck to dodge the other 19 players, so the game is going well, everyone's having a good time showing off their skills when all of a sudden this mass body of a rock hard gangster's, dressed in suspenders, ace duce hats , with little wooden matches placed on the side with no shirt and suspenders that held up their khaki pants! Most of us saw them and tried to run when one of the Local Gang Members) screamed "Nigga you bet not run!", at that point , they surrounded the field and trapped us in. It was frightening to see how any man could get so huge in size. Now mind you, we were only 12 and 14 years old.

These guys looked like they had just got out of jail and aged between 19-23 years of age; I remember telling my brother, "Alvin, don't touch that ball Carton", but see, my brother was the best runner, he had the skills to make people miss (his idol was Mercury Morris, of the Miami Dolphins #22). Somehow, Alvin never heard my request and picked up the carton and started running! "Fuck!", was the next thing that came out of my mouth, sure enough, these Local Gang Members, half man half monster, began chasing Alvin, and just like all the other kids in the neighborhood, Alvin made one miss, then another, and all the other kids who stop playing began to root and cheer for Alvin. I Guess you know this infuriated the(Gangster's) ! Once you reach the end zone, then you're free, that's the rule , you can no longer touch the runner! Well no one told the gangsters that they had to play by the Rules! so one of them Decides to take a full on top speed Run at my Brother! Grabs my brother and drives him into the ground! Mind you this is a 22 year old thug with all this Mass Drives my 11yr old Brother in the Ground like a little Chihuahua ! My Grandmother and Mom always Instilled in me to always Protect My Brother even if you have to Die in the Process!! So all the Gangsters found this to be Hilarious!! All i can say is I completely Blacked out!! I ran over across the field and with all i had Hit this Punk Ass right in the Fucking Eye

ANTHONY BROWN

with a left Swing! All i could see was him dropping and his homies saying ! ooh!!

Shit! Little Man Stole on (Meaning sucker punched) Compton Gangster !! from there the fight was on!! The Gangster gets up and we Start Scrapping!! By this time i tell Alvin to Run! Go Home! Needless to say he Didn't Hesitate! Scram!! His Ass was Gone! At fourteen i never thought about the age Difference i just kept seeing this punk Ass Dog My Brother and because of this Visual i was actually whipping His ASS! Well his Homies didn't like what they were seeing so one of them (Gangster)would tag team and jump in! well because of the flow of my punches i was getting the best of the second guy! by this time the neighborhood had come out to see all the fuss, Cars had stopped, people came outside to watch but nobody called the Cops or tried to stop it or offered to Help! I was on my OWN! Suddenly one of the Gangsters said low Bridge his ASS!! i didn't know what Low Bridge his ASS meant so i just kept scrapping! i quickly found out what it Meant! The third Gangster got behind me and went down on all four's(Elbows and Knees, Like Doggy Style)while the guy i was fighting would push me over the Bridge, Sure Enough it worked! when i fell there plan worked they were able to take advantage and started to deliver some Bomb shell punches! It was by God's Grace and instincts i was able to turn and Run!! I survived ! I was Thanking God the whole time; After getting Home I open the door to find my Mom Passed out, Because it fell in the Middle of the week we had ran out of Food Stamps and didn't have much to Eat, I ask Alvin was he ok? He said he was fine he ask me if i was so ok, I said yea I'm cool when i turned to look at Him he bust out laughing and Said DAMN Tony Man!! What they hit you with!! I said why!?? He says you look Fucked Up! Your Jaw and Ears Make your Shit look like the Star Wars (YODA!), See like i said earlier Alvin always thought Shit was Funny! I said Man! I said to him I'm glad you see shit funny! this Shit Hurts!! As i was putting on an Ice Pack, So Alvin and i both look in the fridge only to find Syrup and some wheat bread, Back in those days if you had the two combination you would just make syrup Sandwich along with a little Kool aid that was left over to drink. After that things began to cool down for me and my Brother. My reputation grew even more around the Schools and the neighborhood, we were able to come and go without any issues! After a few Months my brothers Dad decided it was best for him to leave Compton so he sent for him to join him in Minnesota, it was Heart Breaking for the both of us because we were always together ,the day he left we embraced each other with a Hug! It left a big hole in me because now 'I'm stuck in Compton by myself, i wanted so badly to get on that plane with him- To get out of the Hell Hole.

As time went on i began to adjust to life without Alvin, Word in Seattle from other family and friends that Calif was the place to be- It had sunshine, Women and plenty of Money and opportunity , before we knew it other family members started to flock and make the trip to the land of milk and honey, A Good friend of the family name Lloyd and his older Brother Name Ronald who were Actually from Tacoma Wash, came down to California, they were brothers of my Aunt Eloise Boyfriend name (Daryl), Lloyd was 19yrs of age and Ronald being an Ex-Con who just got out of Prison (Typical Prison Built, 20inc Arms and no legs, Skinny). My Mom said they could stay with us while they got on there feet, So here they come, It was actually refreshing having an older brother type around to learn from, Lloyd help fill the void left from the departure of my brother, We would play Dominoes with the (Local Gangsters), walk to the store without getting jacked because of Lloyds presence , my Mom also enjoyed having them both around because of the protection she felt, things couldn't be better , Well Ronald being an ex-con was attracted and drawn to the streets and Nightlife, He would always be out late which was not good in Compton because whatever your looking for you'll find along with trouble attached to it, so a few Months would go by and sure enough just as predicted Lloyd Brother would find trouble! He comes home one night bruised and battered he had a knife womb right in the center of his stomach. Lloyd ask what happen!!? He said he was jumped by these street Niggas!! he goes on to name a few of them: One of the names he remembered as Butch! I repeated! did you say Butch!? I was like Ooh Shit! i know him- i went on to say Yea he's friends with my Mom and everyone in the neighborhood knows Butch, See Butch to was an Ex-Con, he got out after a five year sentence unlike most ex-cons Butch was slender built, dark complexion and had smooth facial features,(Real Similar to Denzel Washington), word had it he was deadly with his hands (See back in those days there were no drive by shooting - you handled your dispute's Toe-Toe)so as weeks go by Lloyd and i were playing Dominoes when the conversation opens about the situation with Ronald, Lloyd comments were Tony people around here don't really know me and have never seen me Fight!!

Now mind you Lloyd is only 5'7 and weighs only 145ibs so I'm thinking to myself Damn Lloyd how you gone have any chance against these Niggas from Compton, i didn't say nothing when he said that about his fighting skill , i just kept playing Dominoes , so all of a sudden my Mom comes in the Kitchen! she says Butch is down Stairs with his Boys saying he heard you (Lloyd) were looking for him,- Lloyd ask is he outside now!? My mom says yea he's in the front of the Apartment now smoking- Him and five guys- Lloyd says come on Tony come with me just before we go out his brother Ronald comes thru the door but Lloyd never told Ronald where he was going, on the way i pleaded with him- Saying look Lloyd Man! please don't fight this Dude. I love you like my brother lets just forget it!!Lloyd was so confident he says to me Tony you gone see today!! So we arrive in front of the apartments and sure enough there's Butch and his five of the scariest dudes you ever want to see, Three (Gangsters-,Butches Brother (Who was a Former Marine) and this Dude name (I won't say his name!)-(A Notorious street killer that everyone in the Neighborhood Knew) So they face up! Both engage in a very low toned exchange! Butch says so i heard you looking for me!? Lloyd says that depends on if you were the ones who jumped my brother Ronald, Now mind you all these Guys were 6'0 and taller Lloyds only 5'7- I was so proud of Lloyd because he was showing no fear! So Butch Response was ooh you mean that Nigga From Seattle! Well if that's your brother then you can get what he got! Lloyd in a calm voice said fine! Butch puts Down his Cigarette and the fight was on!!Lloyd strikes first with a kick to Butches Balls Butch comes back with and i Mean the Fastest most Devastating Punches had Ever in my life seen, He threw a five Punch Combination that just about knocked Lloyd out! Butches Friends Smirked and said ooh!! Butch is going for an Early Knockout tonight !! at Least so they thought, Lloyd came back with Three shots of his Own that Rocked Butch! As i write this Story I still get goose bumps just thinking about it I've never seen a street fight like this! Man!! back and forth they went at it for at least 15Mins then all of a Sudden Butch began to tire and Lloyd took advantage! he grabbed Butch from behind and snatched his balls and pulled his head backwards causing Butch to be short of breath! His Boys who were standing by began to panic!!they were in total disbelief ! how could this 5'7 Nigga from Tacoma be out here whipping Butches Ass!! they started saying Butch if you don't kick his Ass then I will, Butch started making these sounds like Ahh!! This Niggas Got my Balls Man!! Ahh! Shit!! It was clear Lloyd Really began to pour it On ! Butches Ass was All but Whipped ! The Pride Of Tacoma was Well Represented ! Well this didn't sit well with Butches Brother who was Watching! he said to Butch Again if you can't Kick his Ass i Will so he Jumped in and started Whaling away on Lloyd! by this time Lloyd was Exhausted He (Lloyd) screams !! Tony go get Ronald So Off i went! I ran up the Apartment Stairs and yelled at Ronald! There jumping on Lloyd! Ronald didn't ask any questions! he grabbed a Knife and jetted down stairs! to find the marine on Top of Lloyd! Ronald didn't hesitate he swung the knife at Butches Brother who was on top of Lloyd! he then chased one of the Gangster who made the mistake of falling Down, Ronald stabbed him at least five times, by now Butches Brother

ANTHONY BROWN

Yelled at me " Tony Don't Get In This" Stay out of it! so i did just what he said, I stayed out of it, by the time all this was over Ronald had stabbed Butch four times, one of the Gangsters five Times and got the remaining guys at least twice! the Craziest thing to this is All this Shit was for three Dollars!! See the dope game hadn't hit Compton that hard just yet, people were surviving day to day three dollars could buy you two tall cans of beer; the ghetto choice at that time was Colt -45, Olde-English or Schlitz with your change you had enough to buy a pack of cigarettes and a big Mac so those three dollars were a very big deal (three Dollars would stretch far) it was a Frightening sight! Somehow Butch as well as all the guys survived! no one Died! but guess you Know Shit had hit the Fan!! Lloyd went to jail only to have gotten re-leased six Months Later, Ronald left and went back to Tacoma because word on the streets was the bounty's were out on Lloyd, Ronald, Myself, and My Mom along with my new Baby brother that My Mom had just given birth to, So one day the apartment building was having a block party with people coming from all over from other neighborhoods as the people began to drink and smoke (Weed, etc) the (Gangsters) had confirmed the bounty that was out was on us ! So now I'm Livid!! I'm like I wasn't in that Bullshit! Butches brother told me not to get in it and I Didn't!! What the fuck are they talking about!!?? They were say-ing Yea! Nigga you in it and that Nigga Lloyd and tell your Mom Watch her back because she's in it Too!! I'm like My Mom Fed all you broke Ass Niggas! Gave You all a few dollars when you needed it! What the Fuck!!So in order to keep the party nice and flowing I backed off and told Lloyd later that night what was said, I never said a word to my Mother, So Months go by as I'm doing school going back and forth when guys would come up to me saying " Your Punk Ass gone Die! Bitch Ass Nigga ! you and your family! I'm like Damn to myself! I kept saying I had nothing to do with this ! So one Night my Mom ask Lloyd and I to go to the store for her to buy some Cigarettes and to bring back a Colt 45 Beer- It was about 8pm that Winter night when we went- We get to the Liquor Store with no problem, seems like a quiet night in Compton all is well so on our way back from the store we here a group of guys talking in the streets, we weren't sure who they were so we took the liberty to peek thru some bushes to see who they were' Sure enough it was the Gangsters! The same one's who told me at the block party they had a bounty on us! (Three well known Killer Gangsters) and Seven Others, Ten in All once we spotted them we decided to just hide In the Bushes until they left, Suddenly the chatter had stopped, I'm thinking to myself NICE! We can finally go home and get out of these bushes- So we climb out thinking the coast was clear not knowing them niggas was still in the streets, the reason they had stopped talking was they were full of Wine and Beer, By this time it was too late! They had spotted us when one of them said! There that Nigga who stabbed Butch! And his little punk Ass Brother (Meaning Myself) Lloyd said to me Tony just keep walking and don't say nothing- just keep walking! So I did just That! Well that didn't stop them from Approaching! All ten of them began to draw nearer, I'm saying to myself Damn here we go! So one of them comes straight at me and to this day I still can't make out what he was! He looked like Half Man and Half Reptile! So this thing starts walking next to me and starts putting on his leather gloves asking me what set I was from! ? I just kept walking saying to him I'm not from a Set (Meaning Gang) at that moment I could hear Lloyd saying Tony just keep walking! By this time Lloyd had falling behind me and was totally surrounded by these killers! This mammal was Persistent and wouldn't let up! He just kept pursuing me saying What set you from !? I'm like why don't this guy just leave me alone!! Then I ask him Man! Ain't you about thirty years old ! ? I went on to say I'm only 15 years old man!! Why you want to fight me?? Well dude wasn't listening! It didn't matter to him what age I was! It was either I square up or get sucker punched! So at that moment I Said FUCK IT!! Being Scared to Death and not knowing if I was going to live or Die I just decided Man! FUCK this crazy Ass looking Half Man Half Creature!! So we square up in the Middle of this cold Dark street in Compton! I started my Boxing Technics by

ANTHONY BROWN

bouncing on my Toes (In Boxing this is called Dancing) for rhythm! Measuring the distance of this Gangster!_ He starts to charge forward! That's Where he made his mistake first was leaning forward and throwing this wild right hand and missing! What he didn't know was I was left handed and had boxing experience! I quickly countered his wild right with a devastating left to the Nose and a quick over hand right !! This Combo dropped this mammal to knees where he would grab me by the waist and tried to hold on and twist me down to the ground- I began to pound him in the head when suddenly I hear the sound of a click!! It was a switch blade that another Gangster had and was walking towards Me! I won't try to sound like a Hero and say I stood there like a Man and kept fighting ! I didn't! I got the fuck up out of there! I pushed this falling Gangster (Mammal) off me a Ran like my Ass was on Fire!! Zigging back and Fort Presenting a Difficult target for anyone to shoot me! In the meantime all I could see was Lloyd curled up like in a ball just taking a dreadful beating!! Lloyd did this in order for me to get clear before he got out and Ran for himself He cared that much for me that he took an Ass whopping just so I could get away! We both made it back home Alive!! thank God ! Once arriving my Mom looked at my shirt and ask what happen!! ? I didn't notice the blood all over my shirt from the Gangsters face, I at the time was too scared to notice , Even though we made it back safe my Mom gets mad because we dropped her Cigarettes and beer saying God Damnit!! Go back and get my Cigarettes and my colt 45 Beer- Shit! That shit cost Money! I'm like Mom they mite be Coming over here and start shooting us!! Just as I say that we here a yell outside or door, One of the Gangsters saying! Yea! that's where they live at!! I look outside the window and see at least 20 gang members ! Myself and Lloyd Quickly covered the window with bed mattress to prevent getting shot-we turned off the lights and we all got down on the floor ,See in those days Cops wouldn't come out unless someone was Dead or badly wounded, the damage would have to be done in order for them to come out so we stayed on the floor all night watching the door hoping they wouldn't kick our door in. I literally thought my heart was going stop!! to this day I have never felt my heart beat so hard and fast! Night came and went with us all waking up still alive!(Lloyd, Myself, Mom and new baby(Brother), Lloyd ended up Spending another six Months in jail before being released they (Courts) Realized it was Ronald who did the stabbing thus releasing Lloyd, though things had prematurely seem to have quiet down the word on the streets were any one who seen us were to report to the Gangsters in order to immediately expel us! See all this made no sense to me because Butch wasn't even a gang member! He just hung out with them, It just seem that these guys were just looking for an excuse to get there street credentials , I can remember at least twice a week being told I was scheduled to die because of what had happen to butch. (MY LAST WEEK IN COMTON!!) so on this particular day Monday a group of Boys I knew had pulled me to the side saying – Look Tony Man we like you but if I were you I wouldn't come to school this Friday Dog because I heard these Gangsters Niggas saying your going to Die, Please man don't show up to school, at this point I was completely tired of all this Shit and with this Compton Life! All I use to say was Fuck Compton and just excepted my soon to be Fate! I just said I'll be better off anyway so Fuck It!! I Told my guys I knew (Notice I didn't say friends- Didn't have any!) So tell these (Gang Members) I'm not running I'll Show up Friday! So Monday goes by then Tuesday, by the this time my feelings for life and all my emotions had left, I never told my Mom because I didn't want to have her worried, the closer it got to Friday the MORE INTENSE THINGS GOT I would be in school with a blank stare my body was there but my Soul and mind was separated, Wednesday came and as I walking to school I see these two black guys in the middle of the side walk working on a bike, like they were changing the tire or fixing the flat, I wasn't sure it just looked suspect to me but I just kept walking but as I drew closer I saw one of them looked up and caught eye contact with me he had a mad frown on his face I knew then this wasn't good just as I got inches closer the frown faced guy stood up and started to run towards me I didn't hesitate and

ANTHONY BROWN

I took off I mean I jeted out, swerving thru cars and dodging thru houses just to get away from this guy by this time his friend who was with him was in fast pursuit and I mean fast, I couldn't get enough distance from them because they were faster runners then I so as I'm dodging them I see this open corn field see in Compton they had a lot of horse ranches and wheat and corn fields so I decide to run in the corn field in hope to loose them as I'm approaching the field there's a little wooden fence I saw so I ran towards it , it was kind of small so I figured I could clear it so I thought okay cool I will just jump over it as I'm running not to break stride so just like a hurdler I jump with my left leg straight to clear and with my right leg bent that was my form so far everything was working fine until when I bend my right leg I didn't get enough height to clear the fence and as a result it caught the middle part of my leg thus swinging me backwards and hitting my head on the fence and temporarily knocking me out, the guys chasing me some how had lost site of me they were looking thru the tall corn field thinking I was hiding between the brush if only they had look a few feet behind them they would have seen me hanging upside down knock out on the fence in the same manner a slaughtered cow would be hanging in a slaughter house, I guess this went on for five minutes or so I'm not sure because I was unconscious all I can remember was I started to hear this tearing sound like the sound if someone was tearing a shirt or something as I began to regain consciousness I realized that tearing sound was my leg being ripped by this rusty nail that had punctured the middle of my right leg and was ripping thru my flesh I knew it was bad so I didn't look at my leg so in order to free myself I took my left hand and pulled myself up to the point to were I had enough leverage to snatch my leg free from the nail once I separated from the fence I was able to wrap my leg with my shirt I was wearing and got home safe I never told my mom what happened I just said I needed to get my leg fixed needless to say this event was the last straw for me , something just had to change, however the threats didn't stop coming two weeks after this incident I went back to school only to hear the same echo you gone Die!! I just kept to myself and never said anything to anyone most of the time I didn't even remember how I got home- Didn't remember The routes I was taking , basically just walking in a blank daze- Here I am at 15 years old with all this pressure and for what reason? Other then just living in the wrong environment, As I approached home one particular Friday coming from school look up at the Apartment building at the second floor where we stayed and see my Aunt who's my Mom Sister, she has a suit case's and a bag- Now let me first describe my Aunt! She has the Body of a Young Beautiful thick Country girl, Big Legs , Big Round Butt, Small waist and just 24yrs of Age! Two guys wrecked there cars one time looking at her(So you get the Point on how attractive she was!), On with the story, So as I approach the Door in my mind 'I'm thinking we must be going on a trip or something, just wasn't sure, My Aunt looks at me and said take this suit case's down to the car and sit in there, give your Mom a kiss because your coming to live with me, It was a miracle not only did she save me but I was finally leaving Compton, It was joy and sorrow because the look on my Moms face was disappointing- She was loosing her oldest Son, this leaving her and my baby Brother all alone, It was either stay in Compton and Die or leave with My Aunt and Start a New Life, so I chose to leave with my Aunt! It was the most pleasant ride that I can remember. I huge burden was lifted, I sat quite not saying a word- My Aunt (Who's name is Loise) Ask you Ok? I politely answered and said Yes I'm ok, to this very day never ask her why or what made her come get me! How did she know I was scheduled for execution! See God works in Mysterious ways, _ The Good Lord saved my Life, On the Ride My Aunt Ask me, Tony What do you want to be in Life? To me the answer I gave her made me 100% committed to what my Answered would be, for what she did for me for how she loved me and saved my life, I owed the answered to her, I said Auntie I'm not really good at a lot of things I just know two things that I'm pretty good at and that's Boxing and I'll try football and see which one will make me successful! I gave my Aunt my absolute Promise to fulfill my words to her for what she was doing

ANTHONY BROWN

for me which was saving my life, Going into the fall that year it was time to check into High School from the location of where my Aunt Lived (Which was in the Jungle- an upscale part of Los Angeles at that time) the Closest school in the area was a school name Dorsey!!- (Let me first explain Dorsey Alumni ,It's a school that produced several high profile people from congress to high profile lawyers , Rob Kardashian the father of the Kardashian girls, to famous singers, Billy Preston, Jody Watley to NBA Players James Wilkes, as well as having the distinction of producing more players to the National Football League then any high school in the country so now you get the visual of what type of high school this is) back to the story: I knew nothing about the High school and never heard of it, So this is all new to me, because my Mom was still my legal guardian she had to enroll me, so off we went- Once we get there the lines short for enrollment when all of sudden the mass body of students began to roll in- I just don't mean Students! It was like the Hollywood Grammys! Girls were dressed like women, they had pumps, Dresses, nails, Hair whipped up etc, I mean you name it the guys had rollers in there hair, slacks, dress shoes, watches, cars, !! etc, the athletes look like Giants, 6'9- 6'6, I mean they look like men!! So now I'm standing there with my Mom and looking at the way I was dressed with my one pair of jeans and white T-Shirt with one pair of converse, I felt totally out of place, I look at my mom saying Mom I can't come here to this school! She ask in a loud voice!! WHY!!? I responded with I don't dress well enough and I don't fit around these kind of kids- Why did I say that!!- My Mom goes off (Because that's what people did in Compton (Even though my (Mom) was from Little Rock Arkansas she adapted the Compton ways of behaving) , Loud talk and making a public scenes) She response with FUCK These People!! Don't you ever tell me your Ashamed !! You hold your Head Up and Stop Acting Scared!! Well the situation Really Didn't call for the scene she was making! Needless to say it Drew attention from all the students who were standing nearby- I just wanted to leave and never come back but I went thru it and enrolled, So off I went to school the next week- with my one pair of jeans a new shirt that my Mom had bought and my converse tennis shoes (Chuck Taylor's)

that I washed, See because I moved in with my Aunt the county had cut of my Mom's food stamps thus leaving her with less money for my clothes, I swallowed my pride and just dealt with the shame of not being able to dress like my peer's,- again the girls at Dorsey were clearly the most Beautiful girls I'd ever seen!! They Had extremely Nice Figures that even my Aunt (who was nicely built) would admit Man!! Tony these girls bodies are better then Mine!! It was over Whelming . On the third day I can remember walking down the hall going to class when I walked up on these students rolling dice, It took me back to my Compton days when the gangsters would gamble on the corners, the only difference to this was theses players had perm they're hair with pimp socks, shorts (Short slacks) silk shirts! So as the dice game goes on one of the players realizes something was wrong! Hay!! This Mother Fucker Rolling 7's to Fucking Much!! So he snatches the dice and the other players who were standing by realized the Dice were loaded!! Ahh Shit!! I heard someone said! All of a sudden the guy who had the loaded Dice tried to Run- It didn't work because they cornered him and started to beat his Royal ASS from head to toe, It was funny at first but it took me back to my experience at Compton before Anxiety would take over what I was feeling, Seconds into the Ass whopping they decided to throw dude into a aluminum trash can Head first- All I can remember seeing one of his shoe's flew off, His pimp socks had holes in them with his legs sticking straight up in the Air You could hear the trash boy saying! Ahh Man!! Ahh Man! that's fucked up!! Come on Man!! let a Nigga Up!! I cant Breath ! Come on !! When they finally let him out the Trash can it was the funniest Shit I had Seen!! It was the first time I had Laughed that Hard in years!! His Perm was sticking straight up Like a Chicken- His slacks had ripped in the Ass area- Hilarious!!! However the guys who did the beating weren't to thrilled with me watching and said Nigga you want some!!?? I quickly said Ooh- No!

ANTHONY BROWN

I don't! So I jetted off to class! The very next Day I Decided to get to school early- I heard about how good the school Breakfast that was being served (Coffee cakes, Breakfast Burritos, Huge Cinnamon Rolls, Etc!) Man!! The Lines were Practically wrapped around the corner! So I just patiently waited my turn to! Finally try out this delicious Breakfast ! At last I get to the front! The line is still growing from the other students who were in line waiting! Just as I were approaching the counter a student approached me and says ! Hey I'm in a rush

(Farmdale Brother# 1 The Goose) and late for class so he ask if he could have cuts! So I wont be late- I looked up and says Sure (I still had that gullible Seattle Mentality!) go ahead, All of a sudden Five guys began to go in front of me! Mind you they were Crazy Tall- 6'9,6'8, 6'7 etc, I said hay wait a minute! You can't cut like that, seconds after saying that the original guy who ask for cuts held my chest by holding me back, at this point the students who were standing in this long line behind me went OFF!! Saying Hay!! Dumb Ass!! Why you fuckin let those dudes cut in front of you- Suddenly my Compton Street and Boxing skills Began to kick In!! I looked up at the guy who originally ask for cuts, I was ready to start Thumping!! But as I processed the situation I didn't realize how Big this Dude was! He was 6'3(Ht) Roughly 245lbs with a huge Afro and Jail size Arms!

His Eyes were slightly slanted and menacing (Almost Identical to the actor Ving Rhames), So I'm like Fucked I have take this one on the chin! At that moment I could hear my late Grandfather's words!!(Son you may be good but somebody somewhere is always better then you!! And its always better to say there he Go then to say there he lay!! So I turned to the screaming crowd behind me and said well if you don't like it then you talked to Him!! (the 6'3 245lbs guy who was Cutting) of course they looked at the guy and in turn the big man look back at the crowd as to say! You got a Problem!?? From the point all you could here was silence! I then said YEA!! That's what I thought! So I just took being Punk'd that day and walked to class, Later that week Dorsey was having Football Tryouts, They were Posted all over the school- Guys were flooding the Halls and getting the dates and times , Big Guys, little ones , player hustlers types, player from all backgrounds, Asians, whites, Latino, all I could remember was my Promise to my Aunt that I would make something out of myself and make her proud, for not only believing in me but for saving my life, So I ask a player who stood next to me- Asking Wow!! How come so many players are going out for the Football Team!? His response was Man! Have you seen Dorsey's Cheerleaders? I'm like no! He replies well if you did then you'd know Why!! Me being so young and simple said well there just cheer leaders!! So What! The guy then says- okay Dumb Ass!! When you play football you get the girls, that's why all these dudes are trying out!! He goes on to say most of these guys have no intention of making the team- they just want to be out there long enough to hope and catch the eye of these girls, I'm like ooh- now I GET it!! The guy goes on to say Man! if your this slow in the brain maybe you shouldn't try out, Damn!! I couldn't help but laugh- So first day of tryouts I go out to the field where there's at least 150 guys- The players hustler's (Guys with Hair Rollers) a few old guys(dudes who should have graduated) Asians ,whites etc, My first day wasn't hard for me from all my street experience and Boxing- The Competition didn't bother me, So the coach lined all players by there last name first, A-Z me having the last name Brown would be second in line, so there I am in line waiting for exercises to start when another guy also had the same last name (2nd Farmdale Brother) of Brown said to me- Hay!! What's Up!!? What position are you going out for? I remember saying I don't know for sure but maybe Running back- He then says yea me too and by the way my name is Kevin, In my mind I was like you mean your not asking me to fight or my name isn't Gangster this or that?? It was so refreshing, so practice went on for what was called Hell week, Kevin and I would began to develop a player friendship, After practice we would walk a certain way home, we'd walk a few blocks until I would break off and

ANTHONY BROWN

go my own way- Kevin was extremely interesting to me, He would tell me How he was Jewish and didn't come out the house on Saturdays-I'm like Wait!! How are you going be Jewish and your Black! He went on to say I can see you know very Little about Life- Kevin would then go on to say see I'm not worried about making this team because God is with me and God is on my side- I can and will do all things thru him that strengthens me!! Again I found this to be so different from what I was use to dealing with- the conversations were positive and entertaining, Kevin was the first player who befriended me on the team, so as the last week of Hell came to a close I felt I had done things to catch the coaches eyes by hustling and making plays, because of the multitude of players the coach had to make cuts, the day the list came out the coach posted the five pages of all the players who made the team, I was so nervous I just couldn't look, players were walking away cussing (Man!! This is Bull Shit!!) they were saying "they kept that Sorry Ass dude over me" the guys who were cut were going OFF!! See the pain and agony was too much because the cut guys could no longer be in the line to get the Cheerleaders, So a few guys came up to me and ask did you make the Team!? Before I could answer Kevin walks up to me and says see my brother just like I Said God was going to bless me to make this team- I made the cut brother and so Did You!- I'm Like What! Are you Serious!! Man!! Stop Playing! He said Naw Man!! you made It! At this Moment 'I'm feeling on top of the world, It's the first time in several years I felt Accomplished, Something Positive!! So I then turned to Kevin and said well now that we've made the team we can go get these Fine Ass Cheerleaders everyone been talking About! Kevin looks at me and says Damn Man!! No! these are varsity Cheerleaders, They don't date freshman! 'I'm like Man! I bet I can pull one of them!! Just show me where they are! Kevin says okay Nigga I bet Yo Ass Eat cheese when you see them! I say okay Bet!! So off we go to the circle where the cheer leaders were practicing, As we get close All I could hear was them cheering and going over there materials , but I also saw A multitude of a crowd standing around- Player Hustlers, Varsity Football players,

Varsity Basketball Players, Track guys, Security- Etc, 'I'm like what the Hell is up Kev!! Kevin goes Nigga these are not only Varsity Cheerleaders but also the finest and coldest Babes in Los Angeles!! As he said that_ Behold I saw all Ten of Them- I'm like O.M.G.!! the first Cheerleader 5-7, Creamy Brown Skin long (Natural Hair!) Bow Legs that Started from her Ankles, Round Ass that started from her back of her leg, She look like she had slight slanted eyes, All I could do was stand there, I Just Froze!! I couldn't Talk, Life at the point got real serious for Me! Because 'I'm like how can God create a Girl that's built like That!! When she walked she had a very intense switch, Like she was having Sex with every Step!!- I just couldn't take what I was seeing- Every Ball player, every girl and even some teachers stood and watched her Practiced!! The other nine cheer leaders were incredible as well but this one was like from another World!! I ask Kevin What's her Name! Kev Says Jasmine! I'm like Jasmine?? Kev goes Yea Nigga Jasmine!! Kev Says Yea Remember!! You talking all that Shit about how you was gonna pull one of them well here's your chance!! I looked Once, twice, I real- izes these were not only beautiful Cheerleaders but they were like Mature women! I was not only not Qualified but not even on the same planet well just like Kev said I would do I ate Cheese! I was clearly out classed, I was so inspired by what I saw that it motivated me even more to do well in football in hopes that one day I could get on a level and maybe catch the attention from one of these cheerleaders, the next day we start practice for the upcoming game which was a week away- I made first team as a starter as well as Kev, we were both name first string on the freshman team , Things started off great we won our first few games, Life at Dorsey was awesome! The Varsity Basketball team was Predicted to take City that year, Varsity Football team was in First Place, Man! Everything was Good- By Season end I was named Defensive MVP and selected Conference, Kev earned the respect as being a Full time starter as a very tough Ball player, the season ends and our reps were solid, We Decide to attend the Varsity city championship game, Its Cresnshaw vs Dorsey but before the game it was the Battle of the Cheerleaders, The Dons Vs the Cougars Keep in mind these Battles were bigger than the actual game!! Cresnshaw Cheer leaders had a nice Rep thru out the city as the Best and most dominant Cheering squad, these battels are on par with Grambling Vs Southern (Black College) Battles of the Bands! When half time came the crowds would Gather!1 Because they knew it was going to Hit The Fan, This Day Held up to the reputation- Crenshaw girls Hit the floor first! To say they had nice bodies did the story no justice, I mean Strippers couldn't compare to these Girls!! So off they went, Shaking, Twisting, Kicking, grinding, Panty Showing Etc, The thousands of people in the stands went Crazy!! There throwing insults to Dorsey! Disrespecting all the Dorsey fans and the Cheer leaders ,Etc, After 15Mins they Finished ,The crowd erupts! Yea!! Go Cougers!1 Y'all Killed it!! High Five's! Screams! Etc, All of a Sudden the lights in the Stadium are turned off! The crowd Erupts Again! Because they know Dorsey's Cheer leaders are coming next! Lead by this goddess named Jasmine Marie! – You'll hear them Marching and Entering the Arena! The Marching stops! Silence!! Then The Lights come on! And there they are in Spandex tights, Shorts fitted Shirts! And no socks! Just Combat Boots, It should have been Illegal at That time to wear Stuff like that but it wasn't! Off Jasmine and the girls went, Twisting, shacking , Stomping, twerking!! I mean they Had Kill in there eyes! Five Minutes into the contest you could clearly see who had the Best Squad!! As I looked in the stance I saw two older guys who came to the game with there wives were using there inhalers to try and regain there breaths. I looked over on Crenshaw side saw a student Breathing thru a small brown bag trying to regain his breath, before they were finished with the routine the fifteen thousand in the stance were all standing to there feet cheering at the top of there Lounges! Jasmine and the girls tore down the house!! The crowd Erupted!! I have Never in my life ever seen anything like it, Dorsey had beat Crenshaw and thus won the City Basketball Championship that night, It really inspired some of the young players to want to become noticed on campus in hopes to gain the interest of not only the cheerleaders but any of the nice looking girls on campus, I just said to myself there's got to be at least one of these girls I could find who would give me a chance, because after all I did make the freshman team and did establish myself, so I decided to go for it! Even though Kev told me its only varsity players that get the girls and not freshman- I said after seeing those Varsity cheer leaders lead by Jasmine (All that Body)- I went for it, So the next day there was a girl who Sat in front of me that I Had my eye on from the first day at school, She wasn't overly pretty but just perfect for me, Brown Skin- 5'5- 130, always wore a pony tail and always smelled like ivory lotion, She had a beautiful round plump booty and her feet were always properly manicured

Just a Seattle type! Wholesome girl, So its Monday- First day of the week, I'm nervous as Hell! I built up my courage all weekend long to say something to her, She wore a summer dress with sandals and like always smelled extremely fresh, She Sat directly in front of me so it was easy to get her attention, Kev and the boys Sat near near by watching and waiting for me to make my move, Damn!! I'm nervous but here I go- Tap!! Tap!! On her shoulder, She turns around! By this time all of her friends locked in to see! I'm like Umm! My name is Tony and I.. I..(Stuttering like crazy!) Umm I play football and.. like.. want to know what's your name? She looked at me! Now mind you I didn't have a lot of clothes to wear, All I had was a fishers man's Hat (the kind that Gilligans/ Island Had) a pair of jeans , one pair of tennis shoes and a bomber jacket that I wore everyday

So she looks at me with disgust! And says my name is Karen!! By this time I look over and all her friends are frowning and looking to say like REALLY!! So then I say Ooh, that's a nice name (Sounding Stupid as HELL!!), Then i say you think I could have your ! and before I could say number she put her hand out as to say DON'T!! She goes on to say please STOP! And no! you cant have my number!! Chuckles! I then looked over at Kev and the Boys who by this time were in tears with

ANTHONY BROWN

laughter!! I felt so Ashamed and embarrassed ! I felt like just walking out the class and never going back!! felt Like I was a nobody! After about 15 mins of ridicule and blunt of Jokes I just Sat there just like Charlie brown would

Kev Came over and like a good Friend would do- He gave me words of encouragement ! He said see I told yo Ass! These girls Don't Fuck With Freshman- You Have to be a Varsity Player- I'm Like Why? Kev says because there looking for a Star who's going somewhere, Freshman don't have a future but a guy playing varsity has a chance to go to college- I'm like wait! Girls are gold diggers at this Age!! Kev goes on to say = Yea nigga that's how the game is played and that's how life is, He goes on to say once you make Varsity you'll see!- You wont have to ask for a date! These Heffas will be begging you and not other way around! I'm like (Bet!)-(Bet was a saying at the time to confirm your agreement) See being teased and rejected penetrated me to my soul! That's all I had experienced so far in my young Life, But I completely understood where Kev was coming from, So the next Summer Varsity tryouts were coming up, Sign-ups came the summer of 1977- I didn't grow much-Height(5'8- 165Lbs) is what I hit the scale, Players were coming in at 6'5. 6'3. Etc- I'm like good Lord! I never seen young guys who looked like this, I mean they had beards, Height- Weight, This Shit is crazy! Am I really going to risk my life doing this!! But because I gave my word to my Aunt to either play Football or be a Boxer and make something out of myself- I stayed Committed- So we sign up and head to the field, All 80 or so players, When we get to the practice Facility the lineman had Already started the try-outs, All we could hear was this Commotion – Rip!! Pow!! Thud!!- Fuck You This and Fuck you that!! We look over to the field and all we could see was Dust Flying! Grass being uprooted from the ground- Bodies Hitting the ground!! Were like What! the Fuck is going on out there- It turned out the O-Lineman were trying to block and contain this D-Lineman Name (L)Goose, They were sending three Lineman to block Him- He's Standing (Ht)

6'3- (Wt) 250Lbs, 19 inc Arms a Huge (Hair) Afro with a back pony Tail (Looking Crazy as Hell!!)and Mean as Hell, As the rest of the players looked on fright came upon us!! Were like Man!! Hell Naw!! Im not going out their! If this is what Varsity is about then Hell Naw ! I'm Out! Suddenly as I looked closer I looked at Kev and said Hay!! That's the same Dude who cut in front of me in the lunch line last year- Kev said he didn't cut- He Punk'd yo Ass and took what he wanted, We both laughed! As (L) came off the field we somehow made eye contact- I'm thinking ooh now here we go again!! Is he going try and punk me again? Damn- With All the other players standing by I just can't have this dude try nothing- So here he comes off the field , Shirt torn from the try-out, Blood coming from his right, and left Hands Bloody, Dirt in his Hair with Half his shirt torn, (L) looks at me then Smiles!! You see me out there Fucking these Puck Asses up!! Dumb Ass Niggas!! Thought they could Deal with Me!! In a Loud voice- Niggas IM THE GOOSE!! I'm like Yea Man I saw you!! You was Knocking the Bull shit out them O-Lineman! See I was more Relieved he didn't try to punk me again like he did when we were freshman, I was like whatever you say Man!! From that very moment Lionel and I just began a close Brotherhood!! It was like we were Brothers from another Life- We would lift weights late at night in his Mom's house, See once Lionel makes you a friend you can't have a better person in your Corner- So for Months we would go Late at night to lift weights, 12am-3am I think what really brought us close was the conversation I had about Lionel's Dad, he shared something with me the was very personal ,in the seventh grade year Lionel had transferred from one junior high to Audubon Jr High(Los Angeles, California) making friends came pretty easy for Lionel but somehow he would always feel lost and couldn't quite explain his feelings suddenly everything would come into focus. This one day in particular was a very special day at school. It was Father Son day so upon arrival at school he noticed all his friends were proudly walking with they're dads headed towards the location where the event was to take place Lionel was waiting outside by the playground

ANTHONY BROWN

area near the courts to where he could see his Dad pulling up we'll time was going by and his Dad was nowhere to be found, he had a couple of his friends would come over to check on him to see if he was still coming Lionel would say Yea he's coming he's running a little late he convinced himself that he was but really deep down inside he knew his Father wasn't going to show but if he did show up things would go back to the way they were when they're relationship was on good terms ,Lionel spoke of the days his father would work him all day like one of the workers his dad hired and worked them to exhaustion , it was really ok with him because as long as he was with Dad and was able to spend time with him everything was cool, that's all that mattered just being with Dad! Lionel's Mom however took offence to his father working him all day because she felt it was important to go out and play with his friends and be a boy he needed to just have some fun, what really pissed her off is when she had to fire her own Son because this working all day thing had got old plus the father would never pay him for all the hard labor, he would just buy him something to eat and called it even, he would just drop Lionel off at home and just left after, at this point his parents decided it was best to separate and go their separate ways and live their own lives, so it all came crashing down this father Son Day the love he once shared with Dad was lost forever as he was waiting outside in the yard time was just going by all the boys had there suites and ties on heading in the event Lionel said he was dressed with his tie on with a nice hair cut he had just gotten the other boys kept coming by asking when is he coming ? the event is getting ready to start Lionel would tell the guys with a smile yea he's on his way but deep down he knew that Dad wasn't all the while holding back tears so out of nowhere A coach name Sherrod appeared without saying anything he noticed Lionel's situation. He says (Coach) Come on! I need another Son today would you mind coming with me? When your Dad comes he can jump right in and take over, needless to say Lionel was so happy but still fought back tears at the same time, when it was all over Lionel remembered feeling total hate toward his Dad for not coming and being there for him he went on to say how he just felt lost because he didn't have a father figure to guide him and teach him how to become a man, Lionel had to learn these things on his own and with the help of good friends, see in the urban areas it's a very large percentage of families who are without a Father or Father figure, its very common to see several girls and boys being raised by their Grand Parents or just the Mother often times that's how boys get caught up in the gangs because the gangs would embrace the boys or girls and treat them like a family ,see next to God in the eyes of a little boy or Girls is there Father that's how high a kid looks up to they're Dad- Things were starting to come together with Varsity- The more we lifted the more confident we felt, See practices at Dorsey were like a Lakers game, People would come from all over, Students from other schools, Adults, Parents, This one guy in Particular would all ways be at the practices, Before and after, He stood 6'3- 300lbs, Had a High pitch voice- Look like the genie who came out the lamp! He was much older- like 26 years old, he had no eye lashes and his teeth look like piano keys- But funny as Hell with an extreme gift of Gab, They Called him Ron- Ron was believed to be Gay but he never came on to any of us- So as we go on- Try-outs were Brutal, Hits were extremely Violent, Guys were getting laid Out everyday!! I mean your life was in jeopardy every time you went to practice, As time went on players were being eliminated daily, From Heat, Broke bones or just fear, The Final week of hell week was just about over, Cuts were coming up! At this point I didn't care what was going to happen!! I just wanted this shit to be over- Team or no team, Coaches break practice, They thanked everyone for coming out, They then said check the board If your name is on the list Congratulations for making the team, If it's not then thanks for coming out and better luck next year, Most of the returning guys from the previous year knew they made the team- Average Ht: 6'1 thru 6'6, Weight, 180- 320, the new guys, myself, Lionel, Kev just like the freshman year couldn't look" Lionel was a shoe in- He was named the starter the second he hit the field, Kev and I had good camps but weren't sure- So Kevin goes checks

ANTHONY BROWN

the board, He looks then by his body Language I said well we tried-Fuck It! I'll have to try Boxing or something, He Comes over after looking at the Cuts and says Damn Ton- We gave it all we Had!! I'm like well did we make it !!?? He says Yea I did Ton but your name wasn't up there- I'm like Man! I knew they was going to do that- Man! later for this Team, I was so! hurt and began to walk off!! In a huge Laughter Kev and Lionel both burst out!! Man! yo punk Ass Made It!! We was just playing !! Ha Ha! Ha!!, I'm like Hell Naw!! Stop Playing Man! did i? They Both said Yea go look at the board with yo scary Ass!!, Sure Enough! My name was on the Board- VARSITY ROSTER!! Ooh Man!!- This is the most Exciting time of my Life!!, At that moment myself, Kev, and Lionel began a close Brotherhood! So word got out around campus about the players who made the team, Things started to change the way other students would look at us, I mean it was instant respect from teachers, Janitors, Principles, etc, So one day after practice five of us the newly made varsity players were walking thru the campus- We stumbled on the Cheer Leaders Practice and like always there were a multitude of people crowding around the Rump Shaking twisting—Light, Brown, Dark Skin Cheer leader's, As we continue to walk we noticed two of them looking in our direction, So I say Hay but don't look now but are they looking over at us? (Speaking Of the Two Cheer Leaders) Lionel Says Man! I don't Care About Them Stank Hoes, Kev says Naw they couldn't be-Suddenly two of them stopped cheering and began to walk in our direction, were like Ooh Shit! Damn! Here they come! As they got closer one of them pointed her finger and says come here! All five of us said who Me! That very second one of the players Name Jimmy says Nigga That's Jasmine (Remember Jasmine was the baddest Cheer Leader and Sexiest girl in LA ,) by this time we couldn't Move, I looked at Kev, He looked back at me! I said I think she's talking to you Man! Kev starts to look back with this nervous expression says Naw Man! She's talking to you! (Meaning Me) As Jasmine gets closer she made it clear who she wanted- Him! I'm talking to Him! and pointing Directly at me! I'm like Ooh Shit! This can't be real! Sure enough she says come here, because Jasmine was the captain of the cheering Squad she was use to taking charge, when she ask for something she usually got it, So she repeated and says Come Here!! Referring to me(Tony the Player) I'm shaking like a little Boy who just pissed on himself, so I went over to her! The Boys stayed back, All you could here was Ooh! OoH!! Damn ! He's talking to Jasmine! So as I got close to her I just couldn't look her in the eyes- I was so nervous- I was trembling! She says what's your Name? I said Tony, she then said Yea I already Know- I heard you made the varsity team, I'm like Yea kinda then she squeezed my biceps and ask so you lift weights and before I could answer she says you gone have to be more confident if your going to be around me!! I couldn't say Nothing!! Words wouldn't come out! So I just nodded my head Yes!(Cool) As she walked off I Swear I saw Tadpoles Swimming in front of me, They say you see them just before passing out-It took me at least five minutes before I was able to walk, The Boys Ran over and said Man! What she Say!! At that moment I couldn't Remember! My mind went blank, I was like WTF just happen??This girl just came to me! Out of all the Men in the city- The boys kept asking Man! What Happen!!??- I'm like give me a minute-I'm Shocked right now! So off we went- Practice is going Smooth, Channel 7,2,5 news would be at our practice at least once every 14 days, Fathers would bring their sons to watch, It was almost like being in college, So one day shortly after practice Coach says I need to see Brown, Lionel, James, We looked at each other like what is this all about!?? I'm Like Man! I hope we not about to get Cut, things are just started to be nice around here! Kev says man just think positive- God wouldn't bring us this far to fail, Lionel says see Kev there you go with that bull Shit again, God don't have nothing to do with this, So they start to argue, I'm like OK! Just chill the fuck out- Lets go see what he wants, So we go in the coaches office, Coach says Hay are you boys free this Saturday? We don't have practice so if your not doing anything I want to take you boys to the Dallas Cowboys Boys Practice! I'm like What!! Lionel Says Hell Yea! I wanna go, Coach says Lionel watch your

ANTHONY BROWN

mouth Mattew's! Man! we were excited to see Rodger Staubach, Tony Dorsett, Tom Laundry, Thomas Hollywood Henderson. Man! This is Unbelievable! When we get there, (Thousand Oak Calif) Dallas Cowboys Training Camp, The first person I see is Tony Dorsett- I'm standing next him thinking ooh he's the same size as I am only a little thicker, then here comes Tom Laundry with his Hat, quiet Demeanor and quiet stare, boy we were like little Kids!! Shortly after here comes Rodger Staubach throwing the ball to Drew hill and over in the corner giving interviews was Hollywood Henderson- Man! You could just see by looking at the Boys face (Meaning the Fellow') this trip Had instantly had changed our Life! To be standing there next to Real life Football Celebrities and being out of the inner city and seeing a Different part of Calif that we didn't even know existed Had open our eyes to a new world of Possibilities, Coach then call us over and pointed to this Wide receiver and ask us do you guys know who that is? We all said yea he's a player on the team coach says yes he is but he's also a graduate from Dorsey high! We said what!? Is he really? Coach says yes and his name is Butch Johnson so Lionel goes over to confirm it was true and ask Butch Johnson was he really from Dorsey (High) Butch was polite and says yes I graduated from there; they both started to talk Butch gave Lionel some advice on how to approach the season and what it took in order to become a professional Football player, he says always play for the team but also play for yourself because at the end of the day scouts come to see individuals and not the team Lionel took what butch said to heart and thanked him for spending time talking with him ,The Ride Home was completely silent, Everyone just stared out the car window not Saying a word , upon arrival back at the school we all thanked the Coach and we went our separate ways, the next day at Practice you could tell it had an effect on us, We all had more determination and Focus, Coach even saw the difference in our attitude saying Damn if I knew it was going to have the effect I would have taken the whole team- So the week we Had our first scrimmage game with this team in Granada Hills in the Valley, They had this QB who was supposed to be this hot shot left hand Blond All American Named John Elway- The Name at the time meant nothing to us at the time, I hurt my back in practice so I didn't play Lionel and the boys didn't hesitate to flex there Muscles by completely Dismantling this golden boy- before I knew it the QB had tapped out by the second quarter and was never to return to the game, After the game Dorsey's wreck Grew! (The name we called our Defense) We were the most feared team in Calif, The News were all over us! Everyday in practice the Local channels were at our practice, We were It! The next Monday the starting Lineups were announced, Coach Placed the names on the Board. By this time I had a chance to start (Starting 1st team) to no one's surprise Lionel was every Coaches selection to be the starter, Kev was selected to start a OG and I was selected to start at Strong Safety, Man! This was the life! I was in tears! Just Overwhelm with Joy- just when I thought things couldn't get any better right after practice as were walking out of the gym we run into the cheerleaders ! And who do I see Jasmine!! Now mind you Jasmine beauty and Booming Body was soo developed that it actually overwhelm anyone who saw Her (Older Men, Women, White, Black etc) it was just a gift to look at her from any distance, She was just intimidating , So here she is walking toward me saying I heard the good news- I responded Umm! What good news? She went on to say so you were name a Starter on Defense! I'm thinking like Damn coach just posted the names on the board- How could she have heard of the starters that Fast? So in asking Jasmine, How did you hear that I'm a starter? She answer's in a cute seductive way! We'll lets just say a little Birdie told me- I just smiled- Gave a shy look and agreed , Yes 'I'm a starter, I said well its nice seeing you again and said goodbye- Jasmine then says Wait! Why are you in a Hurry? She then ask me are you busy right now? I'm looking like Damn! I was really just trying to get away just so I could gather myself, I enjoyed the fact the she even noticed me so I answered her and said no I'm not really busy- I was just getting ready to go Home, So Jasmine says I'm really tired of all these boys bothering me so would you mind walking me home today? By now I'm nervous as Hell! Me of all people this broke Ass poor Boy with nothing is getting ready to walk this sent by God Cheer Leader home- So I said yes I can walk you, So off we went, by this time the whole entire team had caught wind of what was happening- So they burst thru the Gym door Saying what the Fuck! This Niggas is with Jasmine Marie. What!! ? All these years I've been trying to get her and this punk Ass New Nigga is with her! They Began to say Man!! Hell Naw!! Some of it was done in laughter and some in jealousy if they only knew how much pressure I was under! But as Jasmine and i continued to walk she starts to ask me Soo tell me a little about yourself? Do you have a girl friend? I answered no I don't have a girlfriend, I went on to say I just live with my Aunt, it's just her and I all I do is go to school and concentrate on Football, Jasmine just responded by shaking her head in agreement, as our small talk continued we final arrive at her house at the front door I gave her the books I carried for her and tried to give her a hug and then just tried to leave to go home- I mean I was already on cloud nine so as I tried to hug Jasmine she says are you thirsty? And invites me in her house " Would you like to come in" I said Yea I guess so! Jasmine then goes in the kitchen and makes me a sandwich and pours me a tall glass of juice, she says here relax and have a seat, I'll be right back! I'm like okay! By this time I'm Like WTF!! How do I deal with all this! As she's walking back to her room all I could see was this small waist and this pear shape Ass with all this hip and sexual body language!! This was way to much for me! But I was also hungry as Hell so that Sandwich was right on Time, So I began to drink the juice and devoured that Sandwich so about 45mins had gone by and Jasmine hadn't come back in the living room now it's starting to get dark I'm like okay I really need to get home, So another 15mins go by and she still hadn't come back in the living room so Finally I get up and head by her room, I quietly call her name, Hey Jasmine!? She doesn't answer, I call her again! Hey Jasmine!? She says Ooh I'm back here1 she says come in I'm in the shower, Have a seat ill be right out! I'm like What!! I'm in Jasmine bed-room and she's in the shower!! Ooh Lord! My heart is surely gonna jump out my chest! This just cannot be Happening! So after ten minutes the shower water stops, Quiet fills the room! I'm sitting on her bed damn near ready to just leave , this pressure was more intense then fighting the Gangsters in Compton- I just didn't know what to expect next, So the shower water stops and the bath room door opens, Jasmine comes out with her bath Robe on and her hair is up in a bun, smelling like fresh soap, Steam still coming out the bathroom door, she softly walks over to her room door and gently closes her room door, she looks over at me and ask how was your sandwich? Before I could say anything Jasmine turns her back to me and slowly takes off her Robe, Dropping it in slow motion! My eyes Popped out of my Head!! My mouth flew Open! At this moment there was no more time to be acting like a freshman, I realized I had to adjust! By the time the Robe got to her Ass! What my eyes saw had pretty much ruin me forever! Jasmine Ass couldn't be duplicated if you were to draw it up from the world greatest Artist! Her legs all the way down to her feet were in poetry form, Her skin tone was creamy brown, she turn to me and gently pushes me down on the bed, she begins to unbutton my shirt and began to kiss me on my neck. Sticks her tongue in my ear and ask me! Are you Cool with this!? All I could do was shake my head! Yes! I couldn't say a word (Nothing would come out), She continues by taking off my shoes, pants and Boxer's(Underwear), she instructs me to get completely on her Bed, which I Did! She then takes complete control, I tried to kiss her just to show I knew how to do it - She wasn't having it! She says Stop! I said okay ,she then continues to message my dick with her hand and at the same time began to suck one side of my chest then the other, This four play went on for at least an hour before she decided to straddle both my feet before she inserted me inside of her, as she began to ride me she has her hands on my chest while she's stroking me! By this time my eyes are Completely closed! I mean by this time my soul had left my body! I was floating in space, She instructs me to open my eyes and look at her, I slowly opened them and began to connect my eyes to hers, She ask me do you like this? I responded Yes!, Jasmine I like it,

She says I'm no longer Jasmine to you I'm your baby Now!! I don't know to this day if she was putting a spell on me or Hypothesizing me! All I know is that this loving was so incredibly good that I would have said anything at this point! I just laid there and did actually as I was instructed! guess we went at it for at least 2hrs! By the time we were done Jasmine again being in complete control she gets up , walks in her bath room and comes out with a hot face towel and wiped me down like I was a baby, Her Mom was due to come home soon so I got dressed kissed Jasmine and jetted out! On my way home I honestly to this day don't remember my feet touching the ground, I just seem to just float all the way home, I just kept putting my hands in my pants to smell my fingers in order to smell Jasmine scent! So the next day at Practice I feel these eyes on me so as I look up its Kev, So I ask Umm WTF are you looking at (Laughter!) He looks and smiles, Yea!! Nigga you got some Pussy last night! Didn't you!? I smiled back and ask Damn! Why you ask that!? He goes Cause Nigga yo Ass is always Quiet but today you got all this to say!! I mean just talking yo Ass off! He goes on to remind me Didn't I tell you once we made Varsity the P.... would Come! I just smiled and said Yea Man! whatever! See I didn't want to start by bragging because it would have got back to Jasmine I was telling everyone we had Sex and it would have ruined it for me to get some more loving from her, Once word got out that Jasmine and I were dating my popularity went thru the roof, every girl in the school started to come up to me and ask if it were true? if I was with Jasmine, guys would see me walking in the hall and would whisper! yea that's dude who talking to her," they would say what does she see in him? To tell you the truth I didn't see what she saw in me either this beautiful powerfully built Goddess could have had anyone she wanted, at this point Kev wouldn't let it go , he just kept trying to get some detail of our love making session As we were laughing it up Lionel walks over- looking Serious! He says I'm glad ya'll seeing shit so funny but truth is this game in a few days ain't shit to laugh about! Manual High got this Big Ass 6'4 240 Running back name Charles who's black as hell and he's not Fucking around so I suggest you stop with all that laughing shit and start taking practice serious, We both look at Lionel and said Yea okay Goose- We got you!! So here's Game day! As we Approach the Game Field it looked like a Superbowl! People were standing in Line for at least a block long- Everyone in the City wanted to see this game_ Both teams were Undefeated, 5-0 going into Conference the crowd was packed! The local news were all over the Stadium- Jasmine and the Cheer Leaders were Marching into the beat of the Drums! Intensity was starting to mount- As we Approach the field we took one look at Charles the running back I remember saying! Ahh! Hell ! Naw that can't be Him! That's a grown Ass Man out there! What Prison did they get that Nigga From! He got a full beard! Lionel looks over at me and says- Don't Worry Brothers we Gon Ta-Too his Black Ass!! Sure Enough as the Game started Lionel and the Boys started Hitting Charles from every Angle! Slamming his Ass from left to right- I've never seen a man that Big being reduced to a Rag Doll- It got so bad that the players on Manual started cheap shots at our players after the play was over! Ron (Who was Lionel Mentor) was on the sideline! Gave Lionel the order ! I heard him scream (This High Pitch Voice) LIONEL! I want that mother Fucker out the Game!! Now!! Speaking of the dirty player name Barnes, Barns was another prison escape looking Character who also 6'4 and also with a full beard, so after the next play Barnes decides to challenge Lionel, tries to hit him after the play was over, Lionel looks at Ron! Ron looks back! Tells Lionel again FUCK Him Up NOW!! Before we knew it Lionel throws a Left and Then a Right! To Barnes Head! Whop! Down goes Barnes! When the players from Manual saw that they Folded! We Crushed them that Day, 48-0 Ass Whopping!(Lesson From Ron After the Game!) The crowd goes wild_ Dorsey is Awesome! As the crowd Says!! As were leaving the field and approach the locker Room Ron is telling Lionel Yea Lionel all this Shit is Nice, Everybody is loving Y'all because you Won but the second you lose Not one of these people will be around, They won't even know your Fucking name, That's just how Life is! People are like Groupies, They

ANTHONY BROWN

all want to be around a Winner!! Just then as I'm walking up to tell Lionel good game Ron Looks over to me and says and Youuu!! MR, I'm Fucking Jasmine! Don't get your feelings Hurt thinking she wants you for you! All you are is just the flavor of the Month! She only fucking you because she thinks you can take her out the ghetto! Once she sees you can't or you faulter she going leave your Ass for someone Else! MARK MY WORDS! Ron had a way with words even though his word were Harsh! You could Receive them because he would have a smirk on his face! So off we went! The rest of the Season went well, We Won Several games that year and made the playoffs only to be taken by a team who hadn't lost all year(Bell High). So the following year we Enter our senior year! Expectation were even higher then the previous year were predicted to take the City Championship ! The Summer of " 78" All returning players are starting to report to camp- I'm in the best shape of my life- Working out with Lionel all summer! Lifting weights over his house late at night until 2am in the morning! I mean were putting work in, My promise I made to my Aunt appears to be Manifesting of becoming a football Player and making something of my Life! Everything is really falling into place- This one particular Morning the phone Rings! Like 7am! My Aunt had already left for work, So it was just me at the Apartment, I was really sleepy from the day before so I didn't never answer, but the phone just kept ringing! At that time we didn't have an answering service to pick-up so it just rang and rang- See some rings are different then others! Somehow in my gut I didn't want to answer because the ring felt wrong! So I decided to answer! Hello! It's my uncle! Hey Tony is that you? I answered Yes it's Me uncle! How are you? My uncle gets quiet and says! Son I think you need to go to your Moms house in Compton! I ask why Uncles (By now my stomach got nervous) He repeated- Son just go! At that Moment I knew my Mom was Gone!! I caught the Bus from LA to Compton- I called my Aunt at Work (Who was working at Greyhound Bus Station) and told her to Meet me at my Moms because something had happened, She agreed- It took me 2hrs to get there, - Once I arrived I saw roughly six police officers and a coroner! They Ask are you Tony!? I responded Yes! They went on to say ! It was like his words were in slow motion! I hate to tell you this Son but your Mom has Expired!! Just then one officer Had Brought out my Little Brother who was just 4yrs Old to me- He had a look on his face and said hey big Brother Mommy won't wake up! He went on to say I was sleeping with her and I was trying to wake her up all Morning! But she still sleeping! Can you wake her up for me!1? I just couldn't break down in front of him_ He didn't know our Mom wasn't ever getting up again! So I took him in the back yard just so he wouldn't see them taking her away! I was holding him in my arms and just froze with anger and ultimate sadness! I look over my right shoulder and see the coroner with a sheet over my Mom as they put her in the wagon! I can't explain what it's like to be 16yrs old and watch your Mom being taking away like that and to hear my 4yr old Brother keep asking when is Mom going to wake up!! At that moment every bad and hurtful! feeling that I had about Compton had resurfaced!! It was like a movie that was being played before my eyes- The Dope Dealers, The people overdosing, the gang Members, the Hit on my life, the little clothes to wear, the depression, Fighting and the despair that came from living their (Compton) all those years engulfed my mind and spirit! Anger to the highest level had control over me that very instant! Once my Moms funeral was set which was in Seattle I made up my mind not to attend! I just couldn't bare to see my Mom in that Box! I just Couldn't! MY Family begged me ! Tony! You have to go that's your Mom! You have to show your last respects, I just kept saying I don't want to see my Mom in that Condition! So they put my oldest uncle on the phone who's was an Ex Military guy and someone who I didn't always see eye to eye with!! So he gets on the phone and began to Persuade me to take this trip and show my Respects! I began to tell him what I told everyone Else! I'm not going so our conversation Ended with him saying he was done with me! And he hangs up in my face! My Aunt Loise comes over to me and tells me you have to go! She goes on to tell me its okay to Cry! That's your Mom Tony! You don't have to hold it in!! Because of my Love for my Aunt I went to Seattle! Needless to say once I got in the Church and Sat down and saw my Mom in that Box I BROKE DOWN!! It hurt me to my soul I cried like a baby! Nothing in life got to me like that! NO Punch from Fighting, Football, Rocks in my face (From Rock Fighting!) So the funeral; came and went! Though My Mom Had nothing to Leave me when she left but her passing gave me determination and she gave me Strength! I was even more determine not to let her dying in Compton be for Nothing! I never ask How my Died to this very Day I Still don't Know! I probably should have received therapy but in the black race there is not therapy for our tragedy! You just move on- I see how killers are made now! When things happen to people they need to be talk to! My feelings were gone! I wasn't able to no longer laugh!, things weren't Funny anymore, at this moment I want to acknowledge the leaders of my family who kept us and sustained balance after losing our base and family foundation,(My Auntie Velma, Shelly, Untie Ester, Janet , Evelyn)Back to the story- When people would say its cold outside! I felt nothing! Returning to football practice my Hits had become Super Violent! Even though I kept quiet I was Highly Confrontational if Spoken to wrongly to I never wanted to hurt anyone I was just trying to erased the pain I was feeling - Love Making to Jasmine felt worthless because I no longer felt the same It wasn't her fault it was my frustration about life- Jasmine was a Pisces and there all about Love so it wasn't hard for her to see the change in me- So this one particular game we return to our locker to get dressed we noticed that our lockers were broken into- Our wallets, dressed pants, cash, etc.. As I'm looking thru my locker to see what was missing! One of my teammates name Dino Came over to me and said Hey Brown! Some girl outside the locker room wants to see you! I ask him well did she say what her name was!? Dino says Naw but she has a major ASS!! Like Man!! I said tell her to hold Tight! I'll be their in a minute, So I finally go out there to see who she was! When I looked at her I was like Hello! May I help you!? I ask ? She says well you may not remember me but I just wanted to know if

I could walk you home? I replied walk me home? I said Sweet heart I really don't think we ever met!- She says do you remember when we were freshmen you use to sit behind me and you ask me to be my boy-friend? At that moment it came back to me!! That's the same girl who dished me and made fun of the way I was dressed and had all her friend clowning me!! I was thinking Whoa! I can't Believe she's out here in the cold standing with her books wanting to walk me home! Even though she had a nice body and at one time I was really crazy about her she still couldn't measure up to Jasmine- So I looked over at my teammate Dino who was standing next to me totally naked and listening to the whole exchange, I said to Dino- Hey Man! can you walk her home because I can't do nothing with this! Dino says hell yea Man ! she sits in my history class ! I've been trying to get her for a cool minute, So I then turn to Dino and said okay cool but can you please get dressed with your Naked Ass!! I then turn to the girl who standing there and politely said sweet heart I can't i have a girlfriend already but if its cool with you my friend Dino will walk you home_ She looked Disappointed but agreed- As I walked away it just blew my mind how things could Change!- THE YEAR OF "78"

So going into our last year , Senior Year, We were Predicted by the local news media and the Southern League Commissioners to Win the city and take the State that year, The expectation were very high, That sum-mer before practice was scheduled to start- I just stayed to myself, Really didn't have to much to say, I can remember going to a remote area of the school just to reflect and gather my thoughts! As I'm doing this it was one player in particular who just happen to walk by that I took notice of_ He was Quiet and stayed to himself! He was wide chest Had a Muscular Built and a New Cornerback coming from the Freshman team, I ask Kev who would always come over and check on me_ I ask Who is that guy (Meaning Farmdale boy # 4, Holb), Kev said Ooh Him!?, Kev goes on to say- He's Coming up from Freshman- They say Dude is tough! He was most Valuable Defensive Player on the

Freshman Team, Kev goes on to Ask Why are you asking about him? I answered ! I don't Really Know why! It's Something about Him that I just can't put my finger on! I've noticed Him around campus but I cant figure what it is about this Dude! I ask what's his Name! Kev says they call him Holb! but he's A,K,A,- name Ko- Jack!!?? I'm like what kind of Nic name is that !!?? We both Laughed! So as the Summer Practiced starts Lionel is his old self, Knocking guys out in practice, Kev's doing his thing and I'm doing my thing! We All were returning starters and just like advertised Holbert is the Beast everyone said he was! Fast, Strong and very Determined! The Coaches took noticed and named Holb the starter at right Cornerback, I can Remember introducing myself to him_ By hey my name is Brown welcome Aboard! Holbert was Polite and said nice to meet you and told me his name! So as the season is about to start just as usual the local news is at our practice, Cheer Leaders, Parents, Students, From other Schools – At our Practice field was like a celebrity function, We were the talk of the City_ Game one Approaches, Were All fired up!! Going thru our Pregame Ritual! The wreck Crew!! Game Starts and were Rolling! We go up by 14 points and we think were the Shit! High Fiving! Celebrating !The Works! All of a Sudden a Twist of fate turned in the other teams directions, and we ended up losing ! – 35-14 WOW!! The Stands were Shocked! Our Second Preseason came: We came out with more intensity and more determined , but the same results! We Lost! Third game! Another Lost!!!! The Local Papers READ What's Wrong with Dorsey!?? 0-3 !! WOW! We were still confident it was only Pre-season, When Conference comes we'll just take conference and run the table! Its Freemont- Conference Rival at there Home ! We come out- 14)-0 Halftime ! Were up! Yea Things are starting to feel like old times, Were Excited ! We Got this!! All Of a Sudden Freemont Strikes Back! 14to 14, Game Tide! We go up 21-14 Yea we got this – For Some Reason the ball never bounced our way again- They Score two more TD'S and won 27-21_ We Loose AGAIN! Game two regular Season, Jeff High School Final- 35-14 Lost! The Local Papers Writes ! The Dorsey Don'ts

Lose Again!! Very next Game ! Homecoming Washington High every-one in the Stadium is going wild! Dorsey can't possibly Loose the Homecoming! 19-0 We go down! Before we knew it we Lost every Game that Year! Everyone! We were All Shocked and Devastated over this! We put all our hopes into this Football thing, just hoping to make something out of our lives! It was a disgrace from all the great Athletes who came before us that gave the school the great name and reputation of being winners it wasn't like we weren't trying things just didn't go our way- We all wanted to go to College even dreaming of having a Chance at Pro! We Quickly learned that in this life nobody likes a looser! The Crowds that use to come attend our practices, the cheer leaders , the parents, etc, began to distant themselves from us, Jasmine gradually stop taking my calls as she began to shorten our conversa-tions and would walk away when I would come by, It was our first real life lesson, See none of us Had Fathers in our life, I never even seen a picture of my father, Kev's Father was murdered when he was a little Boy, Lionel Father would always leave him hanging when it was time for father Son Day! Holbert Father always distant himself when he needed help, Holbert has shared a story once about when he ask his Dad for a few dollars just so he could get to school, Holbert says he spent the last few cents he had to catch the Bus to his fathers Job only to receive a Bag of Pennies from his Dad when he got there, So here we are Winless High School Seniors, No Scouts, No letters, No attention from Coaches ,every under Classmen who use to look up to us started to show Disrespect by saying Look at those Sorry Ass Has been's Them Niggas ain't Shit! The only positive we had came From Ron, Who had already warned us about how Life Worked, He ask us All! Soo now what! What are y'all going to do with your live now! He went on to ask, Where are the crowds Now! See boys All people in this World want are winners! See now you can't buy a friend, What are you all going to do?? We all said we want to go Pro! Ron Responded with Pro!!? ? all yall are only 5'8- 5'9, Get fucking Real!! There ain't no 5'9 Pro Ball Players! Wake the Fuck Up! He goes on to say, Go be a doctor. Lawyer,

ANTHONY BROWN

Carpenter, Dentist, I then replied Ron- I respect you and what your saying but when I was supposed to be studying and learning at a school during my young age I had to deal with Bull shit like Niggas overdosing in my House, having to eat syrup sandwiches, fighting (Gang Members) back and forth to school being laughed at because I wore the same shit at school everyday- See Ron the only thing I know is this Football Shit That's it! Besides jobs aren't hiring young black boys anyway! Ron went on to say Well try everything- Just throw things on the wall and see what sticks, So here we are! All four Teammates (Brothers) at that moment we looked at each other and realizes all we had was each other, No fathers, no one who believed in us but us! So the next day we all decided to go to our Coach and ask if he would call any colleges for us- We knocked on his door, Myself Lionel. Holb, Kev, Coach opens the Door- Hey Fellas, what's up? We open up talks by saying thanks for the three years playing at this school and being our Coach but we came to you because we all would like to continue playing football and ask him would you mind calling some schools for us? Dude (Coach) looks at us all with a straight face and says ! Well honestly guys I personally don't think any of you are Good Enough to Play College Football, He went on to say thanks for all you've done for this school but try to go out and find a Job, He says thanks and closed his door! Stunned was not the word for how we looked at each other ,see my promise to my Aunt was now crushed, She worked day and night to provide for me after my Mom Died ,And now I have nothing to show her- Lionel went Off!! He says Fuck That Ass hole Coach! All I done for this fucking School- See Boys when you think about it This Coach has never gotten any player a Scholarship in ten years! He couldn't give a fuck about any of us, Kev jumps in and starts to preach to us about what God can do if we just have faith- Well Lionel didn't want to hear it at the time and told Kev- Man!! I don't want to hear that bull shit Right Now- Before I knew it they started to argue, Lionel tells Kev- Look you little short stumpy Mother Fucker, You could never block me- See Kev was an Offensive Guard at 5'9- So in Lionel's mind how can Kevin make it to college being an O-Lionel, which at the time made sense. I then looked over at Holbert and ask Man what you think? Holb says Brown, Man! I'm scared to death- I don't know what I'm going do! I just have no clue on which way to turn, See we had made a promise to each other we weren't going to sell drugs, we weren't going to gang bang, Shoot, Stab Rob or murder no one- See Kev talked about how God would Bless us if we just Believe kind of hit home, So at that moment we decided to reach out to colleges our selves- The Following week myself Kev and Holb ask the coach if we could get copies of game film in order to send out film, Coach says sure and gave us the keys to the film room, Great! We all now have hope and a plan. So we get to the film room, All three of us, we couldn't find Lionel at the time so we went on our own- Once we get their we here strange noises coming out the film room- I ask hey fellas did Coach say if anyone was using this room before he gave us the key? They both said no! Okay Cool, So we unlock the door and to our surprise All we see is a Naked Ass moving at a thousand mile a Minute, Bobby socks and Chuck Taylor's(Tennis Shoes) under this Massive Body on top- Were like WTF!! We turn on the lights and low and behold! Its Lionel Pounding this girl_ were Like Damn Goose- WTF! Lionel says just get out I will be done in a minute!! So we close the door- We all say- Can you believe this Nigga!? Man! he's in the film room fucking while were trying to get our high lite footage- We all start to laugh! When he comes out the room we said to him, Damn man! you got the room smelling like Ass!! Yea Most girls have on pumps and a dress, this Nigga had to find a girl with bobby socks and low top Chuck Taylor's tennis shoes! Lionel with his always sense of humor laugh and says, It wasn't the bobby socks or chuck Taylors I was after! We all laugh and said yea we Noticed! It didn't take long to see just how quickly Ron's words were about how people around you change when the bright lights are off, Girls who use to crowd around you would now hang out with the pretty boys with cars, pagers and Money, We were no longer attractive to the cheer Leaders, girls with nice bodies etc, One of the guys said

ANTHONY BROWN

see!! All these bitches are nothing but gold diggers! That's what they do, Chase after guys who are doing Good, See when we were playing we couldn't get rid of these heffa's, now that our season is over we can't find not one of these bitches! An older Assistant coach standing by heard our conversation and replied, no fellas, that's not it! See black women and Black girls are not gold diggers! There a product of they're genetics and DNA!! Were like What!!?? What does DNA and Genetics have to do with being a gold digger!!?? He went on to explain! See Fellas, Traits are passed down- Some day when you have kids your traits will be passed down to your kids- Were like Yea we get that part- So what your saying is that they're Mommas were gold diggers and now these Sorry Ass Girls are like they're gold digging Mammas- He explains See in a Black girls Subconscious mind she sees you as a leader, a person who's supposed to be in charge A person who is strong. See her DNA and genetics tell her at one time you were Rich and had everything and protected her, She's somehow connected to that thru Ancestry – So when your walking around her loosing and being broke and down on your luck it's a turn off to her, That's why she connects to winners, So don't get mad at her just make something out of yourselves and she'll follow you, So one of the lesser players who was listening to us talk said see that's why I date White Girls and don't mess with the chicken head black girls!! We laughed! But in the back of my mind what coach said made all the sense but that didn't stop the drug dealers and gang members from trying to recruit us, each and every one of us at some time during that year was approached , they wanted us because of our popularity and tough mentality, I think the two worst things that happen to our community that year (1978-1979) was one the showing of the God Father part 1, 2,and three , here's what I mean during the two weeks every night of the God father they would show how the Mafia would operate, Sonny and the family (How Al Pacino would conduct the family business by whacking someone with they're drive by shooting techniques, well when the two weeks of the God Father series was over I swear it effected our neighborhoods- before we knew it the news would come on saying how someone in South Central LA had been shot from a Drive by Shooting, the next week it was two incidents of someone getting shoot before you knew it drive by were happening two and three time a day in the second thing that effect our neighborhoods was the emergence of angel dust (Sherm. Dookie Sticks), it basically change our community meaning the common guy trying to compete in the urban arears, (Los Angeles, Chicago, Miami, Washington D.C) here's what I mean when the dealers from LA who were pushing Angel dust they begin to make a grip of money thus it would make things hard on the working guy who would bust his Ass for two weeks and take his check home to wife thinking he was doing something big, well here comes the angel dust drug pusher he breaks out this wade of money and starts to throw thousands to these women (Shopping sprees , clothes, diamonds , Gucci purse, etc, so with all this the nice looking girl who would have been content with the working man now wants the high profile life the drug dealer is providing, the working man is no longer good enough so she and even the average girls want the guy who can shower her with all the gifts so now the working man is Ass'd out because he can no longer provide or keep up the his new competitor we had one girl in particular that was nicely built(Couldn't hold a candle to Jasmine Marie) so one night we go to this club and we see her long story short we say hello Lionel and myself. See Lionel knew a lot of athletes even though we were seniors in high school so he tells this one girl that a friend of his who plays for the Raiders wants to meet her she responds with no im saying this P…. for this particular comedian/ famous actor Lionel says oh, I didn't know you knew him she replies with I don't but when I do I'm having his baby! We were both like WTF! This poor girl is delusional! Well again the long and short we found out a few years later that she did just that she end up meeting this famous guy who I won't say his name in order to protect dudes privacy and had a kid by him , it was the new way women judged men but not only the dating side it also destroyed the neighborhoods, How it effected some users, There were cases to where a guy would get on angel dust and would climb to a tall building when he gets to the top he takes off all his clothes spreads his arms like a bird and jumps off the building thinking he could fly resulting in him plunging to his death, another case is when cops would get a call about a person on angel dust they would bring out five cops to this one dust addict because they knew he or she would display super human strength to where it would take five cops to subdue this one person who had the capability of breaking the hand cuffs and getting free as for the dealer like the saying goes " For the Love of Money is the Root to all evil" here's the story, they're were five guys we knew who were very close child hood friends they got into the angel dust drug selling business, they got to the point to where they hit it big, driving Mercedes Benz, BMW, one even had a Brown Rolls Royce not to mention all the platinum, Gold diamonds, they had it all until greed slip in, one day three of the guys had went out to make there sells of the drugs when they returned to the drug house the two guys who were inside where brewing up the Dookie sticks(Meaning dipping Cigarettes in the sherm and thus making the sticks well the three guys who made the runs entered the drug house they lock the door behind them and headed towards the back rooms how the story goes is that when they came from the rooms they pulled out guns on the two who were pre-paring the sticks the one guy named Skunk(I won't use his real name) says what yall doing with them guns, the three guys said to his two very close friend I'm sorry Dog but where running shit now! And shot the two friends because they were tired of sharing the profits . I just wanted to share how things went from being a wholesome time period to a complete change in one year, It was because of these types of stories that the fellas decided to say no to all this drug selling and gang bang-ing stuff our love and respect for each other as well as to our families was far to great so we passed-So back to the Story -So later that night we all decide to attend a Basketball game at LA high- Myself ,Lionel, Holbert . Kev, we decide to wear our football jerseys to the game, Probably a bad choice because the students, cheer leaders, and LA high football players started trash talking, calling us losers, " Why y'all wearing them jerseys with your Sorry Ass!! At first we just ignored them but our fellow teammates , Anthony Barber, G. Shipp and Lou (His real name was David, we called him Lou because he was a body builder that looked like the famous body builder named Lou Ferrigno) showed up- It became a problem right away see barber would fight a Lion, he was just one of those types, he wouldn't back down from nothing! I myself really didn't want to engage with all this foolishness but because these were my boy's I was not going to let them get rat packed Shipp wasn't as good but he at the same time wasn't no punk, Lou was body beautiful, He had a Man's body in High school and a Mike Tyson demeanor, so the exchanges began! Fuck all yall motha Fuckers is what barber says!! Shipp added his two cents! Yea fuck ya Mamma!! I'm looking and thinking Umm okay fellas we are really out numbered- we probably shouldn't start nothing out here! Next thing I knew at least 50 dudes stood up and left the LA stands and headed toward our visiting side, I'm like Ooh! Hell Naw, this shit is going down, so we headed toward the exit- Once we get outside four guys in there mid twenties confront us! One had a cigarette the other three had beards mustache's , these were grown Ass men- I'm thinking to myself why are they even in this, they should be at work or something, So lou gets onto a shouting match with the one guy who had the cigarette – they started saying Nigga fuck you, Lou says nigga if you want some! Get Some! Why did he say that!? This guy puts down his cigarette and throws a blazing right to Lou Jaw!! Bam!!- From that point the fight was on! Barber Hit one of the three dudes and dropped him instantly- Gary started swinging lefts and rights! By the time I looked up it was complete Mayhem! The 50 or so guys who came out the stands had reached us by now- All I can remember was just start swinging at who ever I saw! Before I knew it I was corned by four guys! All had knives, I was like WTF! I knew this was it my Ass was gone! One guy was coming fast and furious at me all I could do was think Damn I'm getting ready to Die!! He was about to swing his Knife all of a sudden I could hear was TONY

ANTHONY BROWN

get in the fucking CAR!! I looked and it was Lionel and his girl Avis! They swung the back door open while the car was moving! I quickly threw a move at the guy with the knife and dived Head first in the back seat, Avis floored it and we got out of there! I couldn't believe it, My life was saved that day! So Lionel ask Man! what the fuck were you doing!? I said Man! them crazy Ass niggas Barb and Lou and Shipp got me in some Bull shit! But damn I'm I glad to see yo Ass! Lionel goes Naw Nigga you better thank Avis because she saw you! 'I'm like thank you baby! You saved my Ass today! So graduation approaches and none of us had received any letters from colleges, never the less that didn't discourage us, we just kept believing in each other, I decided I would try my hand at boxing since this Football stuff wasn't working, I called this boxing coach I had worked with a few years earlier in the tenth grade, he was glad to hear from me and excepted my wishes to hit the gym, so he picks me up a week later and takes me to the gym on 78th and Hoover street in Los Angeles, Calif, once I walked in the gym I could clearly see this was serious business! These guys had the look of desperation and anger! I'm saying to myself " do I really want to do this" but because of the failures in football I figured boxing had to have better results so off to boxing drills I went, Coach had me shadow boxing for one hour then I was instructed to jump rope for the next hour after Coach would find me a comparable sparring partner, so after completing all my drills I stop for a water break before taking on this sparring partner I just happen to make eye contact with this older guy, he look at me and ask how old are you? I said 17 sir, He said you seem like a smart young man why do you want to come in a place like this? At this time his trainer was coaching this older guy thru his chin exercises , the trainer had him stretch out on his stomach putting his hands behind his back having all the pressure on his chin for the count of (20), he did this three different sets! I was looking and saying to myself this is the craziest thing I've ever seen, the exercise is supposed to strengthen your chin to help you absorb punches to your chin and face area, so once he was done he ask me again why do you want to come in here ? I said well

I'm just trying to make something out of myself the big boxer went on to say your brain is the most powerful tool you have Son, it's going to take you places boxing will never be able to take you, he went on to say go to school Son and never give up on your dream, this place is for guys who are fighting for there life at the moment his trainer chimed in and said see son a man who uses his hands will never be rich but a man who uses his mind will have unlimited amount of wealth and opportunities because they were older guys I really took to what they were saying see they were father figures types which was something I always wanted just some fatherly advice, so the big boxer ask me so what's your name I said Tony sir he introduced himself as Ken I said it was nice to meet you Mr. Ken and thanks for the advice so myself and my trainer left the gym, On my way back I just kept quiet in the car, my trainer ask me was I alright I said yes coach I'm fine but just thinking, Coach ask what's on your mine I told him what Mr. Ken had said to me coach paused and said well that was really nice of him then coach ask DO YOU KNOW WHO THAT GUY WAS? I said yes that's Mr. Ken, coach said he's not just Mr. Ken but that's the guy who broke Ali Jaw! I'm like what!! Mr. Ken broke Ali jaw! Then it hit me, Wait!! OMG! YEA I know him! I saw that in the papers! WOW! That was really him!! I can't believe this! He was so nice to me! At that moment I took MR Ken advice and never thought about Boxing again, I decided to use my brains just like he said,(later that year MR Ken had become Heavy Weight Boxing Champ!!), So it was Graduation time all the boys had earned there diplomas! It Was great, All the boys walked the stage, see back in those day it was rare that a student didn't receive his or her diploma! Kids just had special focus, for us it was a great accomplishment but at the same time a very empty feeling, None of us had any idea what we were going to do, see the very next day after graduation we as students were quickly made aware of how competitive life was, the nerdy students who graduated a few years before were now GM, and Supervisors, We begin to see that being popular in High School wouldn't save you in the real world we've just entered; Life now was about fighting for everything you wanted (Car, Food, Housing,) just basic life's necessities, for several kids parents would tell them either get a job or join the military or go to Collage do anything but you cant stay here (There parents house) the privileges we once received as an Athletes were now gone, the girls who use to submit to our your every call were going to the guys who had things to offer, that high school popularity was now over, we were in the real world now! So I decided to take a job as a shoe salesmen at a lady shoe store, I had lost contact with my three brothers (Holbert , Lionel. Kevin) for about six Months, on my first day on the Job I was quickly taught the art salesmanship, this full sized girl came in and ask for a particular shoe and wanted the shoe in a size 8, So I measured her foot and noticed she needed a size 10. Well the lady found that to be offensive and grabbed her purse and proceeded to walk out the store but before she got to the door the store manager stopped her and ask the women to have seat and that I was new to shoe selling- he instructed me to go grab the size 8 shoe, so I did as he instructed and brought out the size she wanted knowing it was to small for her big ass foot but before I could walk back with her shoes he stopped me in the stock room and said if you ever loose a sale like that again your fired! He goes on to say that the customer is always right! He lighten the situation with a joke! Saying- we know the big bitch wears a 10 but fuck it! If she wants to fuck her feet up with the eights then let her, so I took out the eights and she bought them, so the next day this beautiful women walks in and ask for these five pairs of shoes- she ask for me in particular as a salesman so I go and get her the five boxes of shoes, she then ask if I could put them on her feet for her, so I did but as I attempted to put the first shoe on she opened her legs!! I quickly noticed she didn't have on any panties! I screamed! Ooh shit!! And knocked over the other boxes of shoes! The other customers looked over at me and said " you need to watch your Mouth MR Salesman! The other salesman looked at each other and just started laughing! Saying that nigga was supposed to be this football player! and he scared of pussy! needless to say the commotion caught the attention of the manager who didn't find the situation funny he tells me I'm not going to keep talking to you either figure things out or you can walk, so by this time I needed some air so I walk outside the store telling myself that this shoe selling shit ain't for me, I was starting to feel like a complete failure, so as I get outside standing there as I look to my right I see this guy pushing a grocery basket- He was stacking them up and returning them back in the store, I'm like Damn dude has some huge Ass arms!! All of a sudden he looks at me and I noticed it was my boy Lionel- He was like Hay! Bro!! so we embraced each other and started to talk! Lionel says Man! This working shit ain't for me! If I don't leave I'ma punch my fucking Manager in the face with one of these can goods! I stared to laugh! And begged him not to do it! Lionel ask me how long you been working here at this shoe selling shit! I said a couple of weeks and I'm already tired of dealing with this! at that moment we both agreed to get back to playing ball. As were talking these high school kids who played behind us the previous year drove up in a brand new (Chevrolet Camaro) and started talking trash about us being has been! Saying look at that nigga (Brown) refereeing to my last name with that monkey suit on selling his little shoes! This infuriated me and Lionel! See even though we lost every game as seniors we were still considered two of the toughest guys in the city, the players who were trash talking us got a quick reminder when Lionel told one of them to say just one more word you punk mother fucker and ill drop your sorry Ass in this Fucking parking lot! So off they went! We both looked at each other and said that's it, Lionel goes back to work and slaps his manager before he quit and I walked back in the lady's shoe store and told the managers I was done and I walked, I remember saying to Lionel, I can't and don't want to be average Goose (Lionel). I promised my Mom and my Aunt! She bust her Ass for me every day just so I can have a roof over my head! She's all I got homie, Lionel says don't worry about it Bro just believe in yourself! I believe in us and don't give a fuck if nobody's us will! We both agreed that somehow we just have to get back to doing what we love, so we decided to follow are

ANTHONY BROWN

dream and get back to playing ball! because we didn't have any real weights or a gym membership we would break in USC weight room late at night! Because Lionel had experience in home maintenance he knew how to dismantle locks so it was easy for him to open USC weight room without being detected , so off we went, late at night some time as late as 1am in the morning, just lifting like mad men, the following night we would run sprints at night in order to avoid the crowd's We were high level determined- See being called loser's and has been fueled us! Making history as the only Dorsey high school Football team to never Win a Game in a Season was too painful to live with, so roughly a few months later we get a call from a coach at this Jr, college asking If myself, Lionel, Holbert , Kevin if we would like to come play for our college, it was unreal! Apparently one of our assistant coaches in high school who believed in us called this Jr College and told them we were great players but just had a bad year It was the shot and direction we were all looking for, A chance to become something and erase that embarrassing year of losing! So off we went, All four of us, Even though we were getting our opportunity entering Jr college was like entering the Lions Den, see only the toughest most determined players make it out of JC, there are no handouts, no agents coming to slide extra money, no assistance from Coaches, if you were lucky you received Financial Aid if not then you worked at night and went to school in the day, we knew this was our last shot at getting to a University, the first day of practice we quickly saw the difference between High School and College, These guys looked Sub-Human- Huge was an understatement, we all arrived at different times that particular day, Lionel and I arrived early while Holb got to practice about 30 mins later, even though Kev was coming no one had see him in a year! So when he arrived we didn't recognize him when he walked up we All said Damn!! Is that Kev! What Happen!? See Kev had completely transformed his body from being a chubby lineman to this chiseled ripped DB, A complete before and after look, we ask Kevin what position are you going play, Kev says DB if Ima go pro one day I couldn't make it as a Offensive

Guard, See because of his faith in God we learned to never doubt him, So first day of tryouts coach had lined us up for 40yrd sprints to see what we could bring to help there School ,Coach says I heard you Dorsey boys could play. Lets see what you got!! So holb goes first, He blazes out! Boom! Holbert is gone but as he's running he starts looking like crazy legs Johnson, - I mean his legs were twisting and dipping- He starting off straight but ended up three yards off the finish line! 4.5(40yrd!) is what the coach said- ! 4.5(40yrds) Damn had you ran straight he would have ran 4.2 (40yrds)So we said Damn Holb Man! Why cant you run straight !?? Holbert came over and whispers to us- fellas don't say anything to anyone when I tell you this but when I was a little boy my legs didn't grow right- the doctor told my Mom that in order for me to be able to walk normal I would need surgery in order to correct it, My Mom didn't have insurance so she just prayed and ask God to heal me! Our hearts were touched when Holbert told us the story! I think at that very moment we all became very close, so the next day we go in the weight room to do the strength test. I felt like I was fairly strong coming out of high school so I get under the bench press and put up # 250lbs ! feeling good about myself because it was one of the best lifts ! Until these two guys walked in the room from Compton, they walked in real slow and didn't say much , So the first guy gets under the bench, Dark skin about 6'1- 225 lbs he puts on 315lbs warms up with 5reps the room went silent! Damn were all thinking he's done until he says okay put on two more plates! # 405lbs one rep then two! Ooh shit! The room goes wild! Were thinking that's it! He says put on an additional two 45 pound plate and two 25lb plate and two 5plate # 550Lbs !! we were like ooh hell naw! Who is this guy! So he lifts the weights brings it down real slow, he paused it on his chest one second and pushes it up! Successful! Silence hits the room as if God just walked in the room! Then his Buddy who was with him gets under the bench and repeats the same feat as his friend only to max out at #500lbs , he looks at me and nods his head, what's up! I look with a grin and said well right about now you and your boy is what's up right

ANTHONY BROWN

about now! He comes over and says may name is Mack and my boy his name Nut and were from Compton! i was apprehensive at first because all my experiences from people from Compton wasn't the best at the time, so I ask him Man! how did you guys get so strong! Are you on steroids? He said man! we don't fuck with that shit! He goes on to say life is mind over matter, you just have to open up your mind and your body will do whatever you ask it, so his homie Nut comes over and introduced himself I'm like hey my man my name is Brown, Nice to meet you brothers, So as were talking Coach yells Ok Guys outside for individual drills, so off we go, Coach says lets go over the ropes drill, Coach wanted to test our coordination, so all the returning players went first, 'I've never seen players with such fast feet, this one player name Charles Hines went thru soo! fast you almost needed a camera to stay with him, player after player went thru the ropes with flying colors, So now it's my turn to show my skill set- see not ever going thru the ropes I had no idea what was in store for me, so I tried to copy and do what the other players were doing , So off I went , I cleared the first rope nice and smooth but by the time I hit the second rope is when disaster hit ,My foot got caught and made me tumble , before I knew it i fell and was tangled up and trapped by all ropes! Of course that brought on a barrage of laughter from the returning players, the trainer had to come and cut the ropes to free me, so one of the linemen who was watching from a few feet away says Haay!! The object of the drill Dumb Ass is to go thru the ropes Not get hung up in them !! Of course being called a Dumb Ass didn't sit well with me! So I said to him come call me that to my face and see what happens- of course being 6'4 he comes over, I'm only 5'9 so the size was clearly in his favor, So he repeated I said Dumb Ass! Before I knew it I swung and dropped him! What I didn't know was this lineman was a Jr college all state Lineman, Blond haired, Blond Mustache, Slender build name Tim Sly- Before I knew it Tim got up from the ground and the fight was on, by this time the whole team had crowded around to watch, Believe me when i say Tim was no punk! He hit me with some good shots and I returned some good shots back that got his attention- After a few minutes the coaches broke it up, After the fight one Player in particular name Gram Harrison came over , He started to laugh and introduced himself as sweet sticking, saying its all about water bound can't swim got to drown! See Gram was another 6'4inc D- Lineman who look Black with slanted eyes, Gram says to me you thought you were gone punk the white boy!!?and started laughing again! He goes on to say this ain't the inner city, They got some tough white boys out here in the Valley, so just letting you know, as he walked the fellows look at each other and said now WTF does water bound can't swim gotta to drown mean! So as were trying to translate " Umm water bound means getting close too the water and can't swim means? As were doing this a retuning player looks over and says " You niggas are remedial !! so he goes on to translate what Grams saying meant! The strong survive and the weak perish on the field! If you can't play and get out on the field you get fucked up!! Get it Now! You Dumb Asses! Were like Yea nigga we knew that! So dude shakes his head and walks off so as the weeks go by it became more difficult to travel back and forth to the city and Valley Everyday I basically ran out of money and didn't know what or how I would get back and forth to practice see my financial Aid was denied and the social security checks I was receiving had stopped because I had sat out the first year out of college so one day after practice I just sat in my car that I bought from selling shoes it was late and I was in the schools parking lot I had no moves to make and didn't have any idea what to do next when suddenly the guy from Compton named Mack who coming out of the trainer's room saw me he comes over and said why havn't you gone home back to LA I told him my situation and that I didn't know if I would be able to continue playing for the team Mack says give me a ride to my apartment he went on to say me, Nut and three other player have a spot near the school why don't you come post up with us tonight and when your financial aid comes in then you'll be able to keep playing, this was so very new to me because with them being from Compton I wasn't sure what to think see Mack didn't know

ANTHONY BROWN

my history of my experience from living in Compton but none the less I gave it a shot and decided stayed over with them that night the very second I walked In they're apartment I was greeted with high levels of respect Nut , Mooch, Willard, And Pat Riley (Not the Lakers Coach) all of them said what's up Dorsey! I smiled and said hey fellas what's up they then said were cooking some spaghetti and we know your ass is hungry so come over here and eat! I was so humbled at there kindness because my experiences in my early years was nothing like this as I share this it touches my emotions! later that night Mack come up to me and says I'm going to be real with you your financial aid more then likely is not coming until late December so if you want just stay here with us we won't ask you for any money just don't bring any dope or drink because none of us do that kind of stuff, I looked at Mack and said I'm not sure if I could ever repay you but if and when my money comes ill give you the whole check Mack said I wouldn't take it he just said bust your ass out there and make it, my eyes Swelled up with tears because my perception of people from Compton had changed I knew then I was just in the wrong situation when I lived there see if it wasn't for those brothers I would never have made it thru that first year of Jr, College ,I was forever thankful to them , like the saying goes its takes a village to raise a child it also takes a village to make it thru life, we all need each other, we made it thru that year Mack and Nut were first team All conference Mack received a Scholarship to University of Utah, Nut received a Scholarship to University of Washington State, Willard went on to San Jose State with Pat Riley going to Cal State Fullerton, Mooch had another year So he stayed behind with us so after the season we decided to put our money together and rent a House, as we start to bring out our things to the place I come across my third grade picture from Compton, I started to laugh at how funny I looked being so young , as I looked closer I saw this kid two places to my left, I said hey Man! this kid looks just like you holbert, there's no way this could be you, look at it this couldn't be you then Holbert looks over at the picture and says what kid!? I then point and says this kid right here (

Meaning the one two pics from me) Holb looks!! And says- Man! That is me!! I'm like what! When ! How!!?? Holb goes on to say Yea I went to Lincoln elementary when I was in the third grade- I'm like Man! I did too and I use to walk after school to see my Mom who worked at this Hamburger spot name Alex Burgers, Holbert says Yea man I use to walk after school there also because My Mom also worked at Alex Burgers- He went on to say Yea I use to walk there with my friend- I'm like wait Holbert that was me who you were walking with!! We use to get Ice Cream from our Mom's !at that Moment we both remembered standing in front of our Moms at Alex Burgers getting free food- It then Hit me! That's why I use to stare at Holbert when we were at Dorsey!! I know knew the Mystery of what it was about Dude I couldn't put my finger on He was my best friend when we were I'm elementary school in Compton. We both Laughed for Days after that! (JR, College Struggles!) after moving into our rented house there was very little Money left for food after paying Rent- We basically survived off eating (Kentucky fried Chicken dinner rolls, top ramen, and Bologna,) we would be at Football Practice light headed and weak from not having much to Eat- See Jr College Football is extremely tough! Because there are no perks! No meals, housing, gifts (Cars, Money, Etc)along with the emergence of all the foreign students who flood the classrooms by taking advantage of the free College education that this Country was providing that things became more competitive , now the Junior Colleges were starting to charge for admissions as well as charging for every unit thus making it more expensive to earn the credits to transfer to the Universities this also spilled over into housing as well as Jobs see everyone in life has to perform and compete in order to survive it's all about only the strong will make it to the next Level!! But we were determine to make something out of our Lives so we pushed thru! However we did have a solid support team Lionel's Mom and sisters would come by from time to time and make us up some home cooked meals see Lionel's Mom was the real Madia meaning she was strong and treated us all like we were her kids see the real word for Madia is

Mother Dear but in our neighborhoods we would say Madia for short she would talk to the boys and just keep things 100 percent real she would say a man should always be self sufficient and never believe a girl when she tells you she loves you she says all you have is the good Lord and your family and your Dog that's who loves you so handle your school and make something out of your lives his Sister Stephanie would chime in and tell us the same things from a women's perspective see Steph had her own beauty salon and would give us free haircuts just so we would look presentable if you didn't know by looking you would think we were all related, Lionel's family embraced us like we were there own his sister Beverly would get so excited when she would she us and will give you her last dime if you need if you think you can play dominoes then please don't play Pam because you will get simply Embarrassed, see this prompted me to think! If everyone thought and treated each other the way Lionel's family embraced and treated us then the neighborhoods where we grew up in wouldn't have so much dysfunctionality, being in College your mind begins to broaden I had read an story about Greenwood Oklahoma in the early1920's , a City somewhere near Tulsa that had flourished to the point they called it the black Wall Street! They had thirty Six (Blocks) of Housing, Schools, Hotels, Banks. Churches, Theatre, Doctor's Offices, Barbershops, Tailors. Restaurants, I can remember thinking these people didn't have nearly the wealth of all the Athletes and entertainers of modern day have but yet they were able to accomplish so much Prosperity, They had a togetherness that Lionel's family had shown us I can also remember this preacher said to us one time when we all had gone to church this one Sunday that i will never forget in sermon he taught " For the Scripture says one (1) man can put one thousand to flight were as (2) men can put ten Thousand to flight, meaning all it takes it two guys willing to stick together and trust each other and they could built enough wealth and prosperity to influence thousands! It may not be on the level of the Greenwood Residents in the 1920's but it could perhaps be a start - Back to the story- One day it was really bad, we had ran out of all the food we bought we had nothing for like five days. Lionel always had a stash of top Ramen in his closet, So one day myself, holb and a teammate name Mooch. (Mooch was a black version of porky Pig/ Rerun from the show that's my mama) Decided to go into Lionel closet to grab a few bags of top Ramen (Noodles), Lionel had been gone all morning so we figured we grab a few bags and buy him some later in the week, as we began to search the closet we hear the front door open with a girls voice, turns out it was Lionel and a girl classmate he brought home Now the house rule was to never enter any ones room with out asking, so when we heard him come thru the door we panicked and closed his closet door and hid hoping he'd leave before noticing we were in his room, we had no ideal what we were in store for next, See we kept the door slightly cracked just so when the close was clear we could make our escape so as were waiting we noticed that the female friend Sat on his bed and began to take her top off and undress we were saying Ooh! Noo! If they catch us were soo fucked! But it was to late! We were trapped! So off they went, Lionel and this girl are going at it! I Can't lie the excitement was well worth the show only problem was that Mooch (we came to find out was a virgin) and had never seen a real live naked women before, His eyes were soo big! It looked like he seen a Ghost, He was breathing ridiculously hard like he need an inhaler, Holbert and I said! Mooch be quiet! Before you get us busted!! He started sweating and kept pushing us from the back! Ooh! This was terrible, not only were we stealing Lionel's top Ramen but now were in his room watching him making out! So finally after two hours they both decided to go take a shower this was our chance to get out of this mess we were in, so we ran out once Lionel and his girl went into the bathroom- We all said damn that was close! As we looked down at Mooch pants Holbert and I noticed a big wet spot in his knee area, so I said Damn Mooch- WTF is that? Did you pee on yourself!? Mooch replied Man! Dog I couldn't hold it!! I replied and repeated ! you couldn't hold your piss!? Grown Ass man pissing on your self! Holbert says (with a smile on his face) tone that's not piss! So I ask

ANTHONY BROWN

then what is it then? Holbert says remember Mooch is a virgin tone, so I said what does that have to do with anything! Holbert says well if it ain't piss then its!- at that moment I got it! I said Ahh! Damn mooch! Really! Holbert burst out in laughter and said that ain't the worst part look at the back of your shirt! I looked and sure enough mooch got that on the back of my brand new shirt that I had just bought! Holbert couldn't breath from laughter! I immediately took off that shirt and trashed it! Lionel Finally comes out of the shower and after getting dressed he walks his girl to her car gives her a kiss and returns back in the house, he says don't think I didn't hear yall asses in the closet! We were like ooh! Damn were we making that much noise? He says hell yea ! so I says man! Big Bro we really didn't mean to invade your privacy but we were hungry as hell and decided to get a few of your bags top Ramen noodles, I went on to ask him Umm dude I notice during your Sexing her you seem to be smashing her like she stole something from you, like you were getting revenge! What was that all about? Lionel goes on to say it's funny you noticed that but yea Brown(My last name) I do have this thing against women, he went on to say when I was like in the 6th grade this older lady who lived across the street from me would molest me after school and during the week ends by making me have sex with her, I said but why you and not the other kids? He says because I was so much bigger then all the other kids they choice me because of my size! So then I ask him then why didn't you tell your Mom? Lionel went on to say if I would have told my Mom she would have Killed that bitch, see this women was my Mom's best friend, we were all like Wow! One of the guys who was over at the house heard us talking says Man! Women are worst then Men! So as our (JC) Football season went on, Lionel was a complete beast, No one could block Lionel or stop him- I was able to crack the lineup, Holb was playing behind an All American name Vernon dean (was later was the starting CB with the Washington Redskins , and won two super bowls Rings) Kev was playing behind another all American who later was drafted to the San Diego Chargers, we won our share of games that year, 5-5 record, the following year ,our (Sophomore year which is Jr College Sr year) Kev transferred to a Christian school in Minnesota, Lionel, Myself and Holbert were name full time starters, we all had developed to the point the LA times had wrote a story about us, I had gone from a 250 lbs bench press to # 400lbs bench press running 4.55. Holb had reached # 350lbs and was running consistent 4.42 Lionel was running with DB's and WR's from the DT position and packing 19inc arms, we had developed in to Beast, so here we are being faced with the same challenge of having in our Sophomore year, to try and Win games in order to catch the colleges attention, see when you loose major colleges and universities won't come to recruit you, they only go after winning schools to recruit players, Holb and I had great starts but, Our first game was vs College of the Canyons- 45-0 Ass whooping, our defense was solid but the offense we had several incoming Freshmen who were a little shell shocked from what they were going up against, second game we win 21-7 East LA ! Great! things are looking up all we need are just a few more Wins and we'll Get the attention from the Scouts, Keep in mind seven (7) teams that particular year (1980) were ranked in the top 7 in the entire country, Pasadena, Bakersfield, Taft, El Camino, Long Beach JC, College of the Canyons, Needless the to say we had our work cut out for us, So third game were battling -7-0 were behind but still in the game by second half the wheels came off and we take another Ass whooping 45-0, from that point one loss turn into another and another before we knew it we lost the rest of our games by a margin of 45 to 48 to nothing! This just could not be happening again!.Not at the most critical time of our Sophomore Year (Jr College Senior Year) but just like our High school senior year disaster hits us for a second time! Even though we lead the nation that year in defensive turn overs it wasn't enough to attract Recruiters they just didn't come seeking us or seeking our services only Sophomore with exception was Lionel, Goose made All American that year which brought in several D-1 Schools looking for his services, Washington State, Univ Of Washington, Arizona, Etc, and then New Mexico State which would eventually became his School of choice, We find out later our Head Coach at that time made a Deal in order to convince Lionel to sign with them, We were so happy for Goose because we felt at least one of us made it out! So off to Las Cruces NM he went, Holb and I both remained in Calif to ponder what was our next move, as life couldn't get any scarier one night Holbert and I were home watching the News when the channel comes and says breaking news! There was a massacre shooting involving local former high school students from Dorsey high at a local Bobs big boy Restaurant! Holb and I said WTF! Who could that be? Turns out that two of our former classmates were involved, My dear friend Lou who was the guy fighting at the LA high Basketball fight was brutally killed at the restaurant the assailant had ordered the customers who were dining in the restaurant by putting them in the freezer to Rob them somehow the robbers decided to target Lou (See Lou was extremely built! Huge muscles but as gentle as they come he Wouldn't hurt a fly!) for some reason to this day I still don't know what exactly happen all I heard was the guy put the rifle to his face and pulled the trigger as it turns out the girl who sat next to us in class was a close relative to the assailants! we both were just stunned because it's was the same spot we use to take our girls at night for dinner! It literally took our breath at the News!! At this time we just had no idea what was next for us until After a few weeks later Lionel called one Morn and said Fellas I got some good news!! He said I told the coach up here about ya'll and they're going to give you guys a shot! Holb and I both were over joyed! See New Mexico State is a D-1 College, We were told from our high school Coach we were to small and not good enough to make D-1or any other College and now here we are on our way to a major college thanks to our big brother Lionel and for him looking out for us- I must say Holbert and I didn't Disappoint- We worked out like Maniacs! In preparation- Once we arrived in Las Cruces, NM we were met by the DB coach, His first response was Hay you guys are so short I can eat peanuts off your heads so he takes us for a tour thru the campus and then thru the locker room, Once we get to the facilities we notice the jerseys were hanging up in front of the players with the names on the back. We see the name Smith, Taylor, Johnson, Brown Adams, We both said to ourselves Haay they have a Johnson and a Brown on there team! So we said hey coach we didn't know you had a Johnson and a Brown on your roster, Coach looked at us both and said! Umm! That's you!! Holbert and I both burst out into laughter! This was Great! Everything about the team was first class, this was truly a school D-1 from the plush carpet in the locker room to the Helmets (Every One of them was brand new). To the trainers room (Ten training tables with certified trainers performing tape jobs before practices,) Jacuzzi world pools tubs for injuries to the food courts (4-5 meals a day), our practiced uniforms were washed before every practice, I mean the school was first class all the way not to mention the per diem checks that was provided before games, just before we were shown the practice field we saw three NFL scouts who were looking at a few returning player from the previous year it was the Oakland Raiders, The New York Jets, Miami Dolphins, at this point our minds were blown away! We were now just inches away from our dreams We had our names on our jerseys already and we hadn't even tested! Boy! When we did test we represented well and kept Lionel's good name because we didn't disappoint, Holbert ran 4.4 (40yrds) Benched 350lbs, Vert_35inc I (Tony)ran 4.54 and Benched 400lbs and vert 31inc, It sent shock waves thru the coaches, they're first response was Hay!! we have to put these guys on scholarship! So our first scrimmage was the Crimson and White offense was Crimson and Defense was White everyone wanted to see these tough guys from Cali I can remember one of the weirdest and strangest plays I've ever in my life being involved in so the offense comes out to run this particular play, Quarterback drops back to pass the Defense drops back into our coverages, Holbert and I are playing the same sides , Right Corner and I'm at the right safety position so as we drop into are zones we noticed it was a screen pass meaning the offense gave the illusion they were going to throw the ball deep but end up tossing the ball short which they did, once we recognizes the play I pealed of the zone area which was roughly 15 yards down field the QB threw the ball to our all American TE (Who Eventually was selected by the LA Rams the next year}, so as I read the play this 6'4 255(lbs) TE was in full stride down the sideline all I could do was take off after him in order to stop the play, now mind you he's in full stride high knees with the look in his eyes he meant business, I'm only 5'9 178lbs but because of my reputation as a fierce hitter everyone on the team was in full anticipation of what was about to happen as I begin to gain ground on this high knee 6'4, 255lbs all American I knew in my heart this wasn't going to end well for me but I just couldn't punk out so I went for it as I approach with seconds from impact the strangest thing happens my right cleat just flew off and I sled five yards from the ranging TE who just jump over me and kept going, now you mite say no big deal your shoes just came off see I had my cleats taped from the outside meaning the trainers tape my foot from the inside and out to secured the cleat and to ensure extra support, the only way that shoe could have come off was the trainer would have to cut the tape off with his special training scissors, the rule in football is to never hit a man below his knees because it could damage his knees and ruin his career! By knowing this in my mind I had to hit him from the waist up! I know for sure had we made contact my teammate would have surely paralyzed me they say we have Angels all around us protecting us daily, I ponded my fist on the ground to show I was pissed I didn't hit him but deep in my mind I was thanking the good Lord for saving me- So far life was a real blast in college, see College will teach you several lessons that will last you the rest of your life, for one, how to critical think and solve problems, how to get along and mingle with other nationalities, and to also Never , Ever, pull a Prank on a bunch of Weed Smoking players especially From Florida and Texas the way Holbert did one night that almost cost him from having to get surgery on his Jaw, So one night Holbert and I were heading to the Cafeteria for late night Dinner but along the way we both decide to stop by the room of a few of our teammates to see if they were going to eat with us, Holbert decides this is a great time to pull one of his famous pranks, see Holbert use to find it amusing to put on this Halloween Costume mask and scare people by putting it on and wait for the perfect moment and scare the crap out of people, so he decided to put on this mask and knock on the door and scare them when they answered the door, We'll I felt like it was a bad idea! I said you know Holbert your my dude but honestly I wouldn't do that shit if I was you! Them niggas Ain't Gonna know what to do when they see your Ass at the door looking like that !Holbert says Naw! I got this! I said Yea! Okay!, so we proceed to the ball players from Florida and Texas! Knock! Knock! They say , WHO is it! I said it's the Cali Boys, Brown and Johnson! Open up! I could here one of them Say! Ahh! Man just open the door, It's the two Square Ass Cali Boys! They not gone hit the Weed no way! Open Up! So the door opens! The Player From Texas name Ron Askew Opens! He says What's up Cali? So at this moment I put my foot on the door to keep him from closing the door once he looks at Holb with this mask! I say What's up Skew! At the moment he looks at me then looks at the guy standing next to me who supposed to be Holbert only to see this bald head white guy looking like Jason from Friday the 13th, So he looks at Holbert ! then looks back at me as trying to process what was happening! He looks at the weed as to say " Damn! I need to put this shit down!, He looks at holb with this blank stare as to say "is it me or is Holbert looking different! At that very second one of the players who was sitting on the bed looks at the door and says! Damn!!! Is it me our is the guy standing next to Brown looking like a fuck up version of Frankenstein! I mean that dude head has a fucked up shape! The other player in the back burst out in Laughter! At this time Holbert and I just stood there motion less until Holbert made the mistake of saying BOO!! To askew! You could see the instant panic on his face, he wasn't sure if he should Run or close the door or swing! So his first reaction was to close the door, we'll that didn't work because I had my foot in the door preventing him from closing it , so his next move he wanted to run but Holbert was standing in his way blocking the passage for his exit, so the Last

ANTHONY BROWN

option he had was to swing with all his mite! And that's what he did! Connecting a viscous right hand to Holbert front tooth! All you could hear was Crack!! Like a jaw being separated from a person Mouth! From that point the players in the room all stood up and said WTF!! There high had quickly vanished! Once askew connected to holb mouth all you could hear Holb saying ahh! Askew man!! Its me Holbert from Cali! Ahh! My Jaw!! Holbert quickly snatched off the mask to show it was a prank! Askew being slow in speech says(This is Askew Country Slang) Holbat Man I'm sorr wee!! Maan!) I didn't know that waz you! Our other good friend Brian Cox who was from Calif (Fairfax High) and in the room at the time had no sympathy for Holbert Saying , Man! That's what your Ass Get! You always trying to scare people with that fucked up mask and now it finally caught up to yo Ass!! (On to Football) as the season progressed myself and Holbert were second string which meant we were on the traveling team ,Lionel was named the starter, this was awesome to see the boys on a D-1 college football team was un real we were Finally something special- Finally!! As the season progressed Lionel grew impatient – See the players who were playing in front of us just weren't worthy of playing time they were getting, I mean we were traveling with the team but we just knew we were better then the guys who were in front of us (A) Bad move on my Part) see there were several players who were on the team that felt the same way, the inconsistency in the way player were selected for the starting lineups weren't consistent with the way we were taught, the way sports goes is that the best player will play in the games if you beat him out in practice or if the starter didn't perform well then the guy who was playing better would got his opportunity, so the way the season was going for instance our starting QB had thrown 23 interception in six games we were in several games because of our defense but the end results would be in us loosing by now most of the players including myself, Lionel , Holbert and our fellow teammate QB Brian Cox got fed up with this see Brian being from Cali also just looked at the situation of why did they recruit me if I wasn't going to get a fair shot ,just to take this back a week prior the coaches had a scrimmage and said whatever QB does the best will run this team so Brian says cool! (Now mind you Cox is 6'3- 215lbs)He was also had a very high IQ for not only football but also for life, Brian and I would clash sometimes because we had very different views on things but at the end of the day I would later think about what his opinion was on the subject we were discussing and it would make since, see Brian would also describe the two of us as Iron Sharping Iron- So Brian says Let's do it (The scrimmage) believe me when I say this competition wasn't close When it was Brian turn he gets under center and goes to work in just 5 plays he had over 200 yard in passing this one particular play Brian launched an 80 yard bomb to this Wide Receiver from Texas named English, Brian threw the pass deep and before the kid caught the pass Cox un buttoned his helmet and walked toward the sideline, he didn't even bother to look to see if the pass was completed, he just knew it was a successful play ! sure enough English caught the ball in stride and scored we erupted on the sideline because we figured Cox had won the starting Job well the next day the coaches didn't think Cox performance was good enough so they chose the kid from the Area(NM) to continue being the starter we later find out from some of the players who were at the time playing other positions that they to were recruited to play QB but were switched to a different position in order protect the local players, Brian said to those players hey no disrespect but I'm a Quarterback and I ain't chang-ing my position for nobody, so myself and Lionel and several other players decided to sit out of practice in protest of all the un fairness and the way the Coaches were treating us so we decided to make the at-tempt to transfer to another school, the biggest mistake I made was calling New Mexico State Rival (UTEP) and ask for a transfer, when I got the coaches from there coaching staff on the phone they said yes come on , we would love to have you, Holbert didn't say anything to any of us he decided it was best for him to not get involved with what we were doing and went on to practice and stayed away from all the confusion , the next day at practice the DB coach calls me out of practice and says that the call i made to UTEP will cost me my time here at this School! So enjoy the rest of the time while you're here, I finished the season by doing well- making good plays and making an impact when I did get playing time but at the end of the season just like coach said I was not put on scholarship, Coach was very fond of Holbert and placed him on scholarship, Lionel was to valuable and head coach who refuse to let Lionel walk, It felt like death to hear them tell me I would not be retained, See we were told if we made the traveling team then we would be placed on scholarship, Needless to say my heart was filled with joy for Holbert, knowing how hard life was for him and to see things finally working out was heart filled after the season , I decided to transfer to a small school in Colorado (Pueblo Colorado) , Lionel and Holbert stayed at New Mexico State Brian had enough of the politics and decided to transfer also to Hampton University in Virginia upon my arrival In pueblo it was received with mixed emotions, during test day i did extremely well while in Colorado, I was named the starter right after testing I ran 4.51 in the forty and benched 400lbs with a 34inc vertical several scouts who were in attendance came over and ask for all my information but it just wasn't the same without my brothers ,So one day i called the Coach at New Mexico state had ask if I could return- He said without hesitation he would love to have me back so I agreed and said Yes I'm coming back This brought extreme joy to the boys because once I arrived back on New Mexico State campus I was In for the biggest surprise! There stood Kevin my brother from Dorsey and Jr Valley College, I'm like what's!! up Kev!! What are you doing here!? Turns out Kev and our high school teammate name James Bridges had transferred from there school in Minnesota to New Mexico State! Ooh! This was it! All my Boys were here! All the guys our high School coach that said we weren't good enough to play D-1 Man!! were getting ready to rock this!- once Lionel sees Kev it was a happy reunion the only problem was Goose (Lionel) still wasn't convinced about his Christian commitment so the few days after James and Kevin arrived Lionel decides to set up an arrangement for Kevin to see one of his girls see Goose was like the campus Mandingo with his Alpha Male demeanor the NM and Texas girls just found him to be fascinating so this one particular night Lionel calls one of his friend that he knew she picks up the phone by saying HI babe what's up? Lionel says I need you to do me a solid she replies sure babe anything for you so he goes on by telling her he has a good friend that hasn't experienced being with a girl we believe he still a virgin so would you mind helping him out ? she replies sure just bring him over and I will do my best, so Lionel tells Kev to come with him let's make a run together Kev replies sure he's not knowing or has any idea what's about to happen so when they arrive at the girls dorm she opens the door with a see thru gown on ! Kev look like wait why is she dressed like that? Lionel says to Kev I will see you in the morning from there the girl grabs Kev hand and guided him into her dorm once Lionel gets back to our dorm he says now watch how his ass is going to change once he gets some so the next morning the girls calls and says hey babe the night was a success but could you please tell your guy to leave because I have to go to class Lionel says put him on the phone so she does he says Kev man! Get your Ass up and get out of there before you get her busted! So Kev agrees and heads back Lionel then says to us now watch how his ass starts changing, I have to admit the very second he walked in the dorm we all noticed it he had a new cockiness to his words (Smile) were a little different his walk kind of changed for a minute also it was something like John Wayne! As practice started James didn't disappoint! His speed and routs had propelled him into the starting lineup, James beat out an All American receiver, (who was later Drafted to the NFL), Kev was making his impact as a hard hitting Safety, I was doing my thing and Holbert was doing his, One day we show up at the position team meeting only to find out all three of us were put on the same side to compete for the same position, we were like WTF!! it got so bad that our coach tells us Hey all you Calif boys stop sitting with each other during lunch, we were all saying to ourselves what! is going on with these Coaches all of a sudden, See because

ANTHONY BROWN

we were all seniors the focus was now on the new recruits and the new players, the feeling toward us was like any little thing we did our coaches didn't like would result in us being kicked off the team or reduced playing time, This was a death blow to our chances of getting film in order to send to scouts or catch the scouts eyes if we wanted to have a chance at going Pro , see we just couldn't return home back to calif as failures, So one day in practice Lionel and this cocky white Offensive-Lineman get into it, they started pushing and shoving each Other when the head Coach looks at Lionel and says if you want to stay on this team you better stop with all this Shit your doing or can just take your Ass back to LA, at that very second the white Offensive-Lineman hit Lionel in the stomach real hard said to Lionel you Fucking Nigger, Normally it would have been no question to what Goose (Lionel) would have done to this guy but that day as we all watched Lionel just walked away without a fight, after practice we all got dressed and walked to dinner, the sun was starting to set as were walking toward the cafeteria , there was complete silence from all of us, As I looked over at Lionel tears rolled down his face, He never said a word, I had never seen my brother like this, I was soo hurt that day! Because I knew Lionel would have destroyed that guy but because of the harsh way we were being treated he ate it!! James bridges was an instant star! His athletic skills put James in the first game vs UTEP as the player to watch, James scored on the first catch he had along with the extra point after the touchdown, the crowd went wild!! We won the game and it was pure excitement the local papers (New Mexico) ate it up! James was in every local paper the next day, Coach had made the announcement the next following Monday James bridges was the starter at WR- the boys erupted with excitement!! Yeah!! Bridge (James last name) see that gave us hope to(Kevin and myself) Holbert was the starting left Corner), that just maybe we too could be a starter if we just kept working hard, so Tuesday goes by, Wednesday goes by now Thursday just two days before the next game so just before practice were all in the locker room getting dressed to hit the field when one of the assistant coaches came in and called Kev and James in the office, First thing came to our mind was ooh snap Kev is probable going to get the start this Saturday, that's why they're calling him and maybe James has another interview with the press, So we head out to the practice field, an hour goes by then all of a sudden we see Kev and James heading back to the dorm The boys looked at each other saying Damn why are they going in that direction? That's weird! So after practice we head back to the dorm only to find Kev and James sitting in a dark room with complete silence, we were like Damn! What happen to yall? Why did you leave practice like that? Neither Kev or James said anything for at least 15 minutes, so we ask again! WTF's going on!! Kev says Man!! Yall not going to believe this shit!! We can't play! We all responded What!!?? Why You can't play!!?? What you mean! Kev explained, See that punk Ass Coach from Minnesota called the NCAA and told them we played in a Preseason game before we left therefore where now ineligible ! At that instant our hearts dropped! James never said a word He just Sat there in silence! I felt so bad for James that day- see I just felt like every time we get just a slight edge something would always happen James was for sure going be a star at NMSU and now it's all over, by this time all the other play- ers from Texas and Florida had stop by to see what had happen, there thoughts were met with disbelief and relief, because James had just took they're thunder and was on his way to stardom! however it didn't seem to damper Kevin's spirits, Kev went on to say – Brothers what God has for you no man can take away- I'm still going Pro!! The guys from Florida and Texas chimed in and said how you gone go Pro Cali with no game film? The went on to rant about Cali(Meaning Kevin) you just a scout teamer! The scouts don't draft scout teamers!! See there was always this rival Between Texas , Florida and California players as to where the best players come from! They went on about you crazy Ass hell! Telling Kev to get real! This went on for about 30mins until they decided to leave and go on the chow! Ooh ! the joke began to pile on when they left the room! Saying yea Calif yo Ass is out of touch! you Strange Ass hell! Then one of the said Yea strange like Doctor Strange

ANTHONY BROWN

Love!! Ooh! They all burst out in deep laughter! Then Lionel erupts and starts in with Kev saying there you go with that shit again!! Nobody wants to hear that bullshit! , So the upcoming weeks we were Scheduled to play the Nebraska Cornhuskers they were Rated the # 1 team in the Country- Practices were high level intensity, The boys were at our complete best! See this was our chance to finally show the world and all the people in our families and Los Angeles that we weren't has been and loser's, to also show case in front of the multitude of scouts who were going to be in attendance, see this team was Coached by the great Tom Osbourne , they had Rodger Craig(Running back) Dave Remington(All American Center) , All American Irvin Fryer(# 1 draft pick New England Patriots), So as we approach the Monday prior to the Saturday match up I was(Tony) was in the rotation on defense, Splitting time with the starters, hob was starting at CB with the Goose also rotating- Boy we were excited !! we just knew we were going to do well!! So Tuesday practice came and went, Wednesdays Thurs, we lit the practices up! Coaches raved about the boys practice all week, So Friday is here, The players who were going to travel had they're traveling bags placed in the locker with they're equipment, when we get to the lockers we see Holbert bag but when I looked over to my locker and Lionel's they were Empty- I said goose (Lionel) did anyone say anything to you? Did you get your traveling bag? He replied no but let's go check the traveling team list, Maybe they made a mistake, Sure enough – our name were left off the list! We were saying WTF!! Is this all about!? So we both go to the coaches office for an explanation, Coaches says Ooh, about that fellas (meaning the traveling list) we decided it was best for the team and that we were taking our best players to Nebraska . Lionel snapped! You White Redneck Mother Fucker !! you ain't got a Mother Fucker on this team better then me!! Goose went on to ask- Then why in the Fuck did you have us practicing like we were going to travel!1? Coach says Ooh we just needed yall to give us a good look in practice! At that point I pulled Lionel away and said Man let's just go! This is soo fucked up! When we walked out of the Coaches office, I just remember felling soo sick that I threw up!! See Lionel and I were two of the best players the school had but in life sometimes the best don't always get a chance to shine, needless to say we got the Shit beat out of us, the Score was 66-0, Holbert showed out! He Had 15 Tackles that game and was named Nebraska all opponent team, Meaning who ever played well against Nebraska would win this award, At this point it was just about us finishing the season, Just to get thru all this bullshit- Word had it that the Administration had grew impatient with the head Coach, the word had it that we (the team) had to win the last four games in order to for him(Head Coach) to keep his Job, Sure enough game #1 coach comes to me and says Brown were really going to need you these last four games- the beauty of this was I was playing safety which was on the same side as holb, Both right Safety and Right Corner, just as advertised we blew it up- beat this high scoring team from Texas, Holbert and I both balled out, Then came a team from Arkansas, we got by them with our second straight win, the third game we blew them out also with one last game to go, we were going to travel to West Texas, I was doubtful about traveling because of what happen during the Nebraska week i wasn't sure if I were going to be allowed to travel but sure enough when the traveling team bags were set my bag was placed in my locker, so we arrive in west Texas it was cold as fuck that night! 10 Degrees- Just before the game they brought out this big Ass Buffalo for a Mascot- I've never seen a Animal in my life that fucking Big!! So the game starts. the hits were Vicious! Holbert and I were at our best- Lionel had enough with the Coaches and decided to sit the rest of the season out and wait until the following season. So the game is Highly contested, Back and forth up until the last two Minutes- I ended up with an Interception, we had the game won but the next play the Texas team scored and Won 31-30. We lost a close one, Sure enough the next day our head Coach was Fired ,Jubilation and cheers went thru the dorms- we were so happy because of the way he would treat the players and coaches that I was going to go over and rub it in the coaches face and ask him (so how does it feel to get treated like this coach?) See we heard the coach was so disappointed at getting fired that he cried and said This isn't fair, And like he always said to us! " Life isn't fair" to no one" And he would always say " All the world wants to know is what have you done for me Lately", As I'm going out the door to go and mask in the coaches face about getting fired Holb in a quiet voice says Tone don't kick a man when he's down , So the season comes to an end, We completed the season as a D-1 lettermen, Something that our High school coach said we'd never do, We were told we weren't good enough to play College Football, Three of us being the height between Ht: 5'8 - 5'9 Lionel being 6'2.5, several players on our team were recruited and drafted by NFL teams, (Fred Young(Drafted by the Seahawks), Leo Baker (Cincinnati Bengals), Kerry Lockland(LA Rams), Bobby Humprey(New York Jets)Etc, see even though we only Won three games our senior class we had exceptional talented players. The coach at the time we found out was told to play the local kids even though they were less talented they had explained why no matter what we did most local players were going to play, (Back to the end of the season) See no NFL scout recruited us, No one mention any of us as prospects, All we were from the coaches were just a few kids from Hollywood Calif, So here we are, with No degree and what seem to be no future, So one day we get a call from this agent in Los Angeles who says he heard about us from a mutual friend who was also an inspiring football player, he asked for myself, Kev. Holbert, He explained to us that he can help us get to the NFL, All we had to do was sign with him and start working out for potential work-outs, Boy! This was great news to us. This gave us Renewed Hope!! WE had a pulse, So we agreed All of us except Lionel See the goose had one more year left of eligibility so he couldn't sign with an agent, So myself, Hold, and Kev decided to sign with him, from that point all we did was worked- out while still on campus at NMSU, So about a Month goes by we decided to called the agent to see how things were going -We got no return call and no response, the next Month goes by and still no response, After the third Month we all decided enough already This agent was full of it so we all

Fired him! What a Mistake that was! Turns out this agent was the Biggest (African American) Agent in LA , (Doc Daniels) He represented just about every big time black athlete in Los Angeles at that Time- So now were on our own which also meant it was time to leave the dorm and head back to LA, just prior to leaving Holbert received a call from the CFL (Montreal Alouettes) for a try-out! Kev and I were like What!!? How did you get that Holb(Dog Team) Holb response was Yeah Cuz!(That's what we use to say to each other when something good happed- Yeah Cuz!) I got a shot- see the boys were so close- It was like when one got something we felt like we all had something- It gave us hope, So Holbert stayed back while at the school while we returned back to (LA) it was very quiet and long subdued trip home for me because I'm returning home with nothing the same way when I went to College, See none of us really knew the importance of truly having a plan in motion, All I had was an aunt who believed in me who lived in a one bedroom apartment, the plan was from the beginning was she worked and I make something out of myself by going to School, I felt again like I failed while ridding back to LA on the greyhound bus, Kev and I parted ways and wished each other luck, a week later Holbert called and gave me the report about the try-out he told me he destroyed the work-out but for some reason they chose this other guy Holbert says but what's crazy tone even though they didn't sign me a scout from another CFL team came over and invited me to their try-out next week (The Winnipeg Blue Bombers) we both got excited and both agreed this would be the one Holb trained like never before, He would train at night when no one was around, put on his Walkman and trained like a prize fighter, See just like myself Holbert didn't have much to fall back on Football just had to work, Jobs weren't hiring us(At least not the good Jobs), We just didn't want to be normal guys or average Guys. So with Anticipation from the try-out at Winnipeg Holb smashed the workout and SIGNED!!- One of the boys made it to play Pro Football! He gave us Hope! See not only did Holbert sign but the Blue Bombers had Won the Championship that year, after all these years of loosing Holbert Johnson was now a Champion! My Aunt Loise who I was living with gave Holbert the praise and was over whelmed with happiness for him? what are you going to do Tony? She says you're a grown man now- I can't continue to carry you, so come up with your plan by next week, I was so encouraged by Holbert success I stared writing NFL teams it was just operating in blind faith because I really didn't know how to get in touch with NFL teams I just called the informdation line and ask for the name of the teams and got there address, I told my Aunt my Plans and without hesitating she supported me, three weeks later I go and check the mail and to my surprise I received a letter from the Detroit Lions! Saying I was invited to a try-out, They were having it in Pontiac Michigan in May of that year, WOW! My aunt and I were over Joyed! A NFL Pro- Tryout! I was the first in my family to ever try out for the Pro's- So off to my training I went from running to lifting to trying to eat right- See back in those days they didn't have personal trainers, you either figure it out on your own or you just fail! Even though I played D-1 Football I didn't have the complete knowledge of how to properly work- out or train for the forty yards, see the forty yard sprint was really the most important drill that scouts want to see, they figure if you can run then we will teach you how to play, so unlike Holbert my first try-out didn't turn out that well Once I arrived in Detroit I quickly saw the difference from the comforts of my Aunts Apartment to how the real the world was, The living condition in Detroit was a lot harder and colder, the faces of players and local residence were highly intense and desperate, This look was frightening ! not mention that it was cold as fuck! So we get to the stadium (took a cab from my hotel to the stadium) the person who was in charge of the work-out called out the players who were on this list- He says if I call out your name you have 15mins to warm up and start your work-out, well having the last name Brown i was up first- so of I went- Ok Brown- Line up for your 40yrd dash! Lets Go!! Well I never got my 15mins to warm up- It was more like 2mins- So I stretched got down to do my 40(Yards) bam!! I'm gone! I felt great, Felt like I blazed it! So the guy says ok Brown stand right here, Meaning the side line- In my mind I'm thinking ooh shit they getting ready to sign me! I must have blazed this 40rty- So they told the next 4 guys who ran after me the same thing- as were standing there and were all thinking Man! Were going to get picked up by the Detroit lions, 15mins later the guy walks up to us and says thanks for coming you can exit the stadium !What you mean!? I ask He repeated- Son you hard of hearing!? Exit the stadium_ I responded Sir can I at least finish the work-out? You only gave me 2mins to warm up before the work-out I thought I would have 15mins to warm -up! He says you got 1min to leave or I'm going to call security, By this time I'm pissed! I said go ahead and call them! By this time the Coach from the Lions looks over and says Haay! Get that Ass Hole out of here! Fuckin trouble maker (Referring to me)by this time my Compton past comes out of me- I said fuck all you punk Ass coaches!! come call me an ass hole to my face! By this time security had came over and escorted me out of the Stadium- Some of the other players standing by said Damn Man!! You got heart- Where you from- I said I'm from Los Angeles- They said do you know who that guy was you cussed out? At the time said no I don't exactly know who he was, they said that's the head Coach of the Detroit Lions,, I ask the guys to forgive me of my language l continued to say all I wanted was a fair shot, Dude(Meaning the Head Coach) didn't have to call me an Ass hole like that , I told the guys who were trying out nice meeting you and I preceded to walk out the stadium, the walk back to my Hotel was about 3Miles I couldn't catch a ride so I just decided to foot it back, needless to say its subfreezing but from the disappoint-ment and anger I didn't feel the cold, In my mind I'm thinking how am I ever going to make my Aunt proud and make something out of the promise I gave her, What can I do other then football to make a living, This football shit is so hard I couldn't tell her what had really hap-pened at the tryout I just told her that the lions said they would call us and let us know who they wanted- once I arrived home my Aunt never Doubted me , She just said keep your faith in God Tony and keep trying- Mean while word came that Kevin had received an invite to the New England Patriots, just Like Holbert when he tried out Kev went into isolation- Just trained like his life depended on it, So two weeks later Kev calls and says he drilled the work-out We were like Man! What happen up there? Kev goes on to explain that when he arrived in Foxboro it was cold like Alaska! Players came from everywhere, Kev tells us he almost walked out the stadium when he saw all the participants , Thousands were in attendance! But because of his Faith In God he wasn't moved by the numbers he says I said a prayer looked at the Heavens and went to work, One drill after another, He explained my feet drills were unmatched! My Man to man coverage was flawless! The Coaches kept asking me my name and where I was from! So after 2hours of drills we were ask to run Forty's, This was not a strong point for Kevin, see being a former Offensive Guard he was never able to master the art of running, so The coaches call his number(See at tryouts your called by a number and not your name) Number #2862 your up! Kevs thinking in his mind as he approaches the line to run his 40rty. If I can just run a good time then my dream will come true! And erased all my doubters , God please help me! Kevs says he's filled with emotions! As he gets close to the line! The coach yells! Come on Son I ain't got all fucking day! So off kev went! As he hit the finish line he said he felt solid, felt like he ran a good time, He looks at the coaches as there looking at the stop watch Kev says the coaches looks at him and says Son you have great feet and technique if only you were faster! They never gave him his times they just said thanks for coming to Foxboro! Kev said his heart dropped , he felt like he was that close, finally a chance to show the world what God can do if you only believe, Kevin never once doubted God he just said a prayer thanking the Lord for being with him and giving him the chance, so Kev gets his things and start to walk out the stadium felling a little down but he just continue to press on, as he took one foot out the stadium a coach runs over to him and says Son you had a Hell of a work-out Your skills were unmatched! He says to Kev do you think you can run a faster 40rty time! Kev says to the Coach, " I can do all things thru Christ that strengthen me" The Coaches says here's my card when your ready call this scout and tell him when the time you when think your ready! At that moment Kev in a loud voice says Praise be to God! For with God all things are possible! Kevin called me soo excited!! Tone (Meaning Tony) Man! they weren't ready for me! I said Man! tell me about it Kev goes on to say –I had the best skills out there, Only one problem! I ask what's up!? He said I have to run another 40rty for them in two weeks, See only Holbert had mastered the 40rty at this time of our careers. He repeats tone if I drill this 40rty I'm on the Patriots!! I said Kev I have no doubt you'll run the times needed- See Kev was the kind of person who would research everything- He knew that if he could just master the formula of running he could beat this clock and thus shock all of Los Angeles and all of them Florida and Texas niggas who teased him while in College So he came up with the step theory for the forty yards – He tells me Tone if I run at least 22 steps every time I can run a 4.5 (40yrds) or better So for two weeks that's all Kev did- Mastered his steps! The day of his scheduled second work-out Kev called me and Holbert and ask to meet him at USC(Southern Cali University)- the work-out was early that Morn, We all arrived at the same time, Kev, the scout, Myself and Holbert and one other person, Kev had a bible in his hands that he brought with him that day, The look in his eyes looked like he had spent time with God, I had never seen that look before on him. It was truly spiritual – So the scouts ask are you ready- Kev says yes sir I'm ready! Kev lined up and took a deep breath and took off- See all Kevin needed was 4.52 and he was a Patriot! See that day God was surely with him because Kev ran a 4.47(40rty) and 4.48(40rty) after the work-out the scout said to Kevin welcome to the New England Patriots our boy did it!! Kev was now A New England Patriot!!) I had tears in my eyes because just like he said all his life, God would Blessed him to become a Pro Football Player! His Dream just became a reality! We both prayed together and thank God for what had just happen- The 2nd Dog (That's what we called each other, Dog Team) team was now a Pro Ball player Kev called everyone to tell them the good news(Lionel's Mom, Ron, My Aunt Liose, etc} Ron got so excited he told Kev to come by the next day so they could celebrate, Kev agreed, so the next day came and Kevin went over to Ron's house, they agreed to meet at 3pm, Kev called Ron and said he's on his way , Ron's says cool, I'll be here waiting, when he arrives at Ron's place he rings the security front door letting Ron know he's down stairs, Kev's just couldn't wait to see Ron's reaction when he sees the contract! He dials the security's number! Ring! Ring! Humm, no answer, Kev tries again! Ring! No answer! Kev thinks that's odd, I just talk to his Ass an hour ago, see back in those days we didn't have a cell phone so Kev decided to walk to a pay phone to call which was down the street, still no answer, the call just goes to voicemail, Kev leaves a message Ron! Where you At? I'm at your spot! Thought we were going to have drinks and celebrate!, so after an hour Kev decides to leave and call Ron later figuring he just got caught up or something, so later that night Kevin called Lionel and ask if he seen or spoke to Ron, Lionel says no he hasn't heard from him but he'll try calling to see if he heard anything, well five days later Lionel gets a call from a detective and ask him did he know a Ron Dorn, Lionel ask why? And why you calling me? The detective tells Lionel Ron has been murdered in a drug heist and that he (Lionel) was suspect in the murder and has to come down for questioning, Lionel is in Shock because Ron was like his mentor and big brother! When he gets down to the station the detective hit Lionel with a series of questioning and show him some pictures of Ron being shot with a phone in his hands with a quarter of a million dollars on his desk, apparently the shooting wasn't about the money, it was about the principle see Ron was a graduate from USC and had an extreme gift of gab! He could convince you of anything, well apparently whoever shot Ron wasn't after the Money they just wanted to send him a message, the story hit the LA times as con man murdered in his Wilshire condo, Lionel broke the news to all of us once Kev found out he was heartbroken telling Lionel that he had just spoke with Ron and that he went over to his house to see him, Lionel went on to tell Kev that he was lucky that Kevin didn't arrive 20min sooner or he prob would have been shot also, see the time of Ron's murder was the exact time Kevin had arrived at Ron's place, it had explained why Ron didn't answer the door, we were not only hurt by Ron's murder but also at the reasoning, see Ron always told us to never ever do or sell drugs and only to find out that he was involved in drugs totally surprised us, So on with the dream to succeed when Kevin arrived in training camp with the New England Patriots he said just like New Mexico State that everything was first class But even more so in the National Football League he called me one day and said man these fans are crazy as Hell. He went on to say they would be outside early in the morning freezing there ass off just waiting for us to come to practice see at the time the Patriots were not a very good team they only had won two or three games the previous year Kevin was telling me that there going to be a dynasty in the upcoming years , this was in 1984 when this happened I said man I don't see it but sure enough just like Kevin said the Patriots went to the Superbowl the next few years (1986) and from that point the dynasty was in effect,, The way things went for me at that point I had several other work-out's even though I didn't Sign or was selected I got better with every outing, A month after Kev signed Holbert had returned from Winnipeg- He got a call from one of his teammates – WR named Jeff Boyd who invited (Jeff was at the time a standout WR who played for the CFL Blue Bombers) Holbert to work-out with him at Rams park with the newly Signed QB the Rams had picked up from Canada (Deter Brock #5) Holbert calls me and invites me to come work-out with him, Jeff, And Deter, I agreed, it was on an early Morning Saturday- once we get to Rams park we meet Deter who eventually became the Rams starter that year, So we start the work-out, it lasted roughly two hours, Holbert was scheduled to return to Winnipeg Blue Bombers to play for them for his second year, the problem was Holbert was now married with a daughter and didn't want to return, so after the work-out we decided to walk over to the Rams office since we were already at the practice facilities, sure enough the DB coach was in the office so we ask the secretary if we could speak to him- Coach agreed to come out to meet with us, so I introduced myself and Holbert as two DB's who were headed back to Canada but before we return were asking if you'll be willing to give us a try-out before we sign back with the CFL, now I knew I didn't have any contracts from the CFL but what the heck, what's a guy supposed to do! What did I have to loose, We'll sure enough it out worked, coach agreed to give us a shot, HE SAYS COME BACK TO Rams park in two weeks and be ready! WOW!! This was it! Holbert and I were at Rams park and now have a workout with the local NFL team, from that point it was all business , Holbert and I went to work, we work-out like never before, No phone calls, no going out, no girls, just all business, the time had arrived, Holbert picked me up that morning and off to Rams park we went, Once we arrived we didn't know there would be # 500 other players they invited, all going out for different positions but because of our prior experience of try outs we were not fazed by the competition- So the try-out starts with one drill after another, Holbert and I had out shinned the competition , 1on 1's, backpedal drills, 7on7's etc, so after two hours we looked around and it was just the three of us Holbert, myself, and coach, Coach stopped the drills and called the two of us over, He Sat down on the ground and remained quiet for at least 10mins! In my mind I just knew we were headed to the roster, Both of us would be Rams! He looked and said you both have done an exceptional job but there's only one problem! I only have just one contract available so you both talk it over and decided which one of you are going to take it! At that moment satisfaction came over me! I finally was looked upon as a Pro Football player but my Love for Holbert and knowing his situation with his family was not even a debate I said to Holbert your going to take this deal, You have to stay in Los Angeles , Holbert and i we hugged each other, we laughed and thanked God for what was happening to us, See that day we showed the locals and all the doubters that we have always been good enough players to play Pro ball

During the Rams camp Holbert showed out from the second he hit the field see from all the experiences of the trials from LA Valley Jr College and going up against some of the cities best players along with some of the Top Guys while at New Mexico State Holbert told us that it was actually harder in College so in his first Preseason Game against the Cardinals coach called Holbert in the game he said he was nervous as Heck but he knew he had a Job to do so on the second play the Cardinals QB at that time had dropped back to pass he looked one way in order to throw off the defense then looked back to Holbert side Holbert said he was waiting because he had a feeling the play was coming his way sure enough the QB released the pass Holbert said everything went in slow motion at that moment he step in front of the receiver and intercepted the pass then took off down the field, he remembered bodies flying all around him trying to tackle him he couldn't hear the crowd because of his adrenalin before he knew it he had ran for 58 yards and almost scored Boy! From this difficult journey of not knowing how life would turn out during high school and not being recruited during College to now making an interception in a National Football League Game we were incredible happy for our Boy, I wasn't sure what my next move would be, there were no more work-outs lined up I just prayed and ask God so what do I do next? It was crazy because one week later I get a call from my dear friend name Brian Cox who was my teammate from New Mexico state that had attended Hampton University and who was at the time was represented by the same agent we both had signed with name Marv Fleming who was the starting TE with the Green Bay Packers who won the first two Super Bowls and also the starting TE with the 17-0 Miami Dolphins- Brian says hey Brown I just ran into our agent at Venice Beach and he ask if we would be willing to play Pro Football in Italy? I said Cox I didn't know they had Pro Football in Italy, I ask how did they know about us? Cox said they saw us at a this-out and wanted to see if we would mind joining them? I told Cox hell yea I'm down Cox says okay cool ill call Marv well just five day after that conversation with Brian I received a call, My

ANTHONY BROWN

Aunt answers the phone saying Tony someone from Italy wants to talk to you!? I said what do they want? I don't know anyone in Italy, I'm thinking it's a bill collector or something! It never crossed my mind it was the scout from the Pro team- She says well there asking for you so talk to him! so I get on the phone and I did what my Aunt ask me to do, Yes may I help you!? He says Hi Tony my name is Vic Desro and I heard you were a good player! The kind of player were looking for! He goes on to say your Agent and your teammate from College Brian Cox referred you as someone who can help us Win games, He went on to say we called the Rams and they gave you a good recommendation so we would like to ask if your interested in playing Pro Ball in Italy! I said I didn't know they had Pro Football in Italy- He replied Yes they do and the Owner is Georgio Armani (the famous fashion designer) I just couldn't believe it! I Immediately Excepted ! My aunt cried! She said Tony I always knew you would make it!! I thanked her for never giving up on me! So Brian and I both were flown over to Italy and we both signed with this Italian team when we arrived in Italy I really weren't sure what to expect in our my mind were thinking this would be easy money seeing that soccer was the big sport in all of Europe but what we wasn't prepared for was that the Italian American Football players had played in the US in colleges and had American Football experience, Just about all of them had played on the Italian National team, we found out quickly these guys were no joke!, they had size and speed with power, Our DT. (Ht) 6'4 (Wt) 325 and ran 4.82 in the (40) Name Pepe Moscatli, Next player (HT) 6'6, WT(265) D.E, Padro Padroni, Paulo Muti 6'4 Wide Receiver, and brother Marco Muti 6'5 T.E, and my very best friend Vismara! Just to name a few, All were National Italian Players with American Football experience! My first practice I wasn't sure if I was at a fashion show or a football club, these guys were coming to practice with Armani suits on, with Beautiful sports coats, hair slick back with moose on and driving Alfa Romeo cars, Mercedes Benz, I mean just dress clean, I'm thinking to myself they can't be that good they look like they should be modeling somewhere, boy was I wrong! When we put on the pads and started hitting I was saying to myself WTF did I get myself into , see with all of my hardships and disappointment prior to coming to Milan it had prepared me to succeed, in life sometimes if you take your rejections and learn from them it could actually be preparing you for success, from all the setbacks from College and the losing all our games in High School and not making it at all the several tryouts nothing they could throw at me mattered nothing would effect my determination , I was prepared for the mental and physical side of making a team the competition was not only from the Italian Players but from the other American players who were flown in , Brian and I were the only players from the west coast most of the other guys were from the Univ of Miami. University of Tennessee, Penn State, Syracuse, Grambling State univ, after two weeks of two a days and three Preseason games I not only made the team but was voted team captain! Brian was traded to a team on the Southern Section of Italy where he excelled and took that team to an 10-4 record and playoff berth my team Went to a 12-2 record that year and made it to the Semi Finals in the play-offs my dream and promise was fulfilled ! I had basically made peace with the sport of Football with all the past failures were now behind me, the Amazing thing was the next year Lionel had received a tryout with the N.Y. Giants under scout Tim Rooney ,Like the boys Lionel didn't Dis-Appoint! He smashed the work-out- The only problem Tim Rooney says to the Goose was we have Four All Pro's at LB. Lawrence Taylor, Harry Carson Harry Reasons, Carl Banks, He tells Lionel go play in the USFL and come back, Lionel does just that- Goose goes to a tryout in Arizona and signs with the Arizona Wranglers, The USFL folded that same year after goose had signed, Holbert went on to sign with the USFL (Philadelphia Stars) Coached by Jim Mora, he also later went on and signed with the San Francisco 49ers Coached by (Bill Walsh) with Joe Montana, Ronny Lott, Jerry Rice Rodger Craig Etc, Kev went on to become an actor, Producer, Song writer after the New England Patriots one of the most beautiful things that happen the day Kevin got

ANTHONY BROWN

married, his Mother couldn't attend the Wedding so for a moment he had no one to stand in for him to represent his side of the family Lionel's Mother caught wind of the situation and told Kevin I will stand in and be your mother, she says your like my Son and she represented him, Lionel went on to work with camera on several televisions sets with several Prominent (A) Scale actors and actress and just like he did when we were in college when he got hired to the very prominent company he pulled each and every one of the boys in and we all got hired , Holbert is a professional trainer working with actors and entertainers he motivates us because he stays in tip top shape and works out Dailey, myself and my partner Brian Cox open a sports agent business called (Top Flight Sports Management) and became sports agents- See we may have not been house hold names or Won any Superbowl but for a moment in time we all became Winners! We are four guys who didn't have fathers but stuck together like bothers and did things the right way and made our dreams come true!! The thing that I'm most proud of is we all are good fathers to our children and are very active in there lives, See we all are born with a gift and talents- The good Lord blessed each individual with something special. I just encourage you to find what your gifts are and go for it! To this very day the boys are still together though we've ventured into various walks of life we see each other every week! There's a proverb that says " If you can find just one true friend in life then you have found something more precious then Gold" we'll in this case I truly can say I'm bless to have found four good friends IM VERY PROUD TO BE APART OF MY SPECIAL BROTHERS AND VERY HAPPY AND PRAISE GOD TO BE CALLED ONE THE," FARM DALE BOYS!!!!"

In Summary! Our story just isn't about football, It's about doing things the right way! See we didn't sell drugs or join a gang or use violence, we did things by working hard and believing in each other, See people always say if you work hard you can achieve what you want, the thing they don't say is that if you work hard that very thing your going after will began and revel its secretes to you thus making it easier to accomplish whatever it is your pursuing, be it a Nurse, Basketball Player, Teacher, Doctor, or wanting to be a Student trying to graduate! ETC, whatever your Dreams are you can become it! Have Faith and go for it!!

"If your weak in a crisis then truly you are weak indeed a true measure of one's strength is not when your Up but its when your DOWN "

What to give a shout out to my extended Family, Lionel's Sisters , Stephanie, Beverly, and Pam! We love you for believing in us!!

~~~

In Loving memory of our Friend, Ron Dorn
Alvin McCoy, (2018)
Louise Darensbourg

ANTHONY BROWN

www.ingramcontent.com/pod-product-compliance
Lightning Source LLC
LaVergne TN
LVHW011410080426
835511LV00005B/467